HOW TO KISS GOODBYE TO ANA

of related interest

I Can Beat Anorexia!
Finding the Motivation, Confidence and
Skills to Recover and Avoid Relapse
Dr Nicola Davies
ISBN 978 1 78592 187 2
eISBN 978 1 78450 459 5

Eating Disorder Recovery Handbook
A Practical Guide to Long-Term Recovery
Dr Nicola Davies and Emma Bacon
ISBN 978 1 78592 133 9
eISBN 978 1 78450 398 7

Rebalance Your Relationship with Food
Reassuring Recipes and Nutritional Support
for Positive, Confident Eating
Emma Bacon
ISBN 978 1 78592 119 3
eISBN 978 0 85701 278 4

HOW TO KISS GOODBYE TO ANA

Using EFT in Recovery from Anorexia

KIM MARSHALL

Illustrations by Hayley Reynolds

Jessica Kingsley *Publishers*
London and Philadelphia

First published in 2018
by Jessica Kingsley Publishers
73 Collier Street
London N1 9BE, UK
and
400 Market Street, Suite 400
Philadelphia, PA 19106, USA

www.jkp.com

Library of Congress Cataloging in Publication Data
Names: Marshall, Kim (EFT practitioner), author.
Title: How to kiss goodbye to Ana : using EFT in recovery from anorexia / Kim
Marshall.
Description: London ; Philadelphia : Jessica Kingsley Publishers, 2018. |
Includes bibliographical references and index.
Identifiers: LCCN 2017041813 | ISBN 9781785924644 (alk. paper)
Subjects: LCSH: Anorexia--Treatment--Popular works. | Emotional Freedom
Techniques. | Self-care, Health--Popular works.
Classification: LCC RB150.A65 M37 2018 | DDC 616.85/262--
dc23 LC record available at https://lccn.loc.gov/2017041813

British Library Cataloguing in Publication Data
A CIP catalogue record for this book is available from the British Library

ISBN 978 1 78592 464 4
eISBN 978 1 78450 841 8

Printed and bound in Great Britain

MIX
Paper from
responsible sources
FSC
www.fsc.org   FSC® C013056

⊪⊪⊪ ◆ ·◆· ◆ ⊪⊪⊪

Anorexia is not about the food itself.

*It's the plateful of fear and
guilt that comes with it.*

⊪⊪⊪ ◆ ·◆· ◆ ⊪⊪⊪

Ana's Calling

I feel in control
When you are around
It's familiar
The only thing I need to understand.

I know what is coming
I know it's all pain
So why would I want to
Go there again?

Cold, tired and hungry
No thoughts of my own
Just trying to get through the day
Leave me alone!

Please tell me how does it stop?
How does it end?
I fought you before
And I can do it again!

But the pattern is there
The urge is so strong
Don't know how much longer
I can keep holding on.

Don't eat! Can't eat!
Someone help me…please!

'Cos I wanna hold my head up high
As I walk through the streets
Not bothering at all
What others think of me.

When I look in the mirror
I want to see someone else
Someone confident
With no concerns about themselves.

I want to feel free
With no worries
Popular, loved by all
But most of all I want to be beautiful.

Contents

Acknowledgements

Thank you to my two beautiful daughters, Erin and Jodi. It amazes me how you have been through so much and, although you have your moments, you have been so brave and just get on with life without grumbling or kicking up a fuss. I am sorry for everything I have put you through but I hope that you know how much I love you and I hope that you are able to learn from my mistakes and live long, fulfilled lives. Remember, girls, that life is short; opportunities are everywhere. Follow your dreams and do not let fear stand in your way.

My wonderful parents, Graham and Liz: Tears are filling my eyes as I write this because how can I ever begin to express how grateful I am to you both for everything you have done for me? I will be indebted to you forever. You are both my rock, the place I turn to when I need... well anything actually. I would be lost without you.

Chris: I only hope you manage to keep reading to Part 2, as this is where I admit that I blamed others, particularly you, for my issues. I know that was wrong and

I had my own part to play. It was a tough time for you having to deal with my illness and your mum's passing. Thank you for supporting my children and for some wonderful times we shared together. I will treasure these memories forever. You will always have a very special place in my heart.

My brother and sister-in-law, Dave and Soph: I am sorry for making you cry, Dave – something you never do, I know. Thank you for making the trek down to Aylesbury with Greg and Alex most weekends and for being there for me and the girls, not only while I was in Aylesbury, but also before and after.

My friends and family: For all your love and support while I was in Aylesbury. I feel very blessed to have you all in my life and I am touched by the generosity that you showed towards me, especially when you had so much going on yourselves.

Kay Lobo: For giving me hope by referring me for residential treatment and providing support afterwards.

The staff at the International Eating Disorders Centre at Aylesbury: You do an incredible job under the most difficult circumstances with the most difficult clients.

Rachel: Thank you for introducing me to EFT. I not only transformed myself but also I am blessed to be able to help others do the same.

Tania: For the outstanding effort you took over proofreading this book.

Dave: Thank you for sending me that song. Thank you for loving me even though I tried so hard to push you away because I was scared. You accepted me for me and loved me anyway. You will never know how special you are to me.

Disclaimer

This book is based on my own experiences of recovery, both personal and professional.

I recognise that anorexia and other eating disorders are extremely complex and do not guarantee results or claim to treat or cure anyone. I teach EFT as a self-help tool and indicate the work that can potentially help in order to quieten the anorexic voice that is so powerful.

I also recognise that barriers to recovery are high and not everyone is ready to do this work. I do not claim to fix anyone; unfortunately I do not have a magic wand. As a practitioner, I can simply walk by your side, supporting you every step of the way.

EFT is a complementary therapy and is not designed to be a substitute for any conventional medicine or psychological treatment. Your doctor should always be consulted in the first instance.

Please note all client's names have been changed to protect their anonymity.

Preface

Amazingly, there is a happy ending to my story that I would never have imagined. I want to offer hope, to encourage and to advise on how to give yourself the best chance to break free. This approach will not be for everyone and maybe you're not ready just now. But I can honestly tell you that it's been the key to my own and my clients' recoveries. Just have a read, do the exercises and see how you get on. What have you got to lose?

Others, unfortunately, haven't had the same happy ending and my heart goes out to their families. It is in memory of those tortured souls that I write this book. I pray that no one has to endure further suffering to the devil in their head. This will be the battle of your life but if you really want to, you can win!

Introduction

Many people who have struggled with an eating disorder have life stories that are full of trauma and negative experiences, and, as a result of these, they became ill. This is not my story. To me, I have the best parents ever who have just tried to do their best. So my childhood wasn't perfect, but whose was? I wasn't bullied at school. I wasn't abused. I did get divorced from the father of my two daughters but lots of people do nowadays. So why me? Why did I become so ill, and why did I get to the point where I thought there was no way out?

The first part of this book is my diary; it explains my story of how every day I felt tortured by the negative voices in my head. Some of it, I guess, makes for tough reading, but I make no apologies for that. 'You never really understand a person until you consider things from his point of view…until you climb into his skin and walk around in it' (Lee, 1991, p.33); and it is the same with any mental illness. You will never appreciate how difficult it is unless you've been there and experienced it yourself.

In the book I mention weights (briefly) and food intake, not to trigger anyone (as I'm well aware this can happen) but to show that you can have anorexia but still eat and not be skeletal. I often denied I had an issue because of both of these aspects. An eating disorder is a mental health issue and, to me, it was the voice in my head that was the major factor.

I hope that sharing my story will help you, as a sufferer of an eating disorder, to acknowledge your own feelings, step out of any denial you have, admit there is actually an issue and know that there is a way out – a way to break free!

For family and friends or for students and professionals, I hope this book helps to provide a typical insight into the mind of someone with an eating disorder.

The worksheets in Chapter 10, quote cards (from the inspirational quotes scattered throughout the book) and daily affirmations (from Chapter 11) are all available for download so you can print them and keep them handy or put them up around your home. Download them from: www.jkp.com/catalogue/book/9781785924644.

PART 1

MY STORY

Would you expect others to be perfect?

No?

So why do you need to be?

Do you feel you need to save the world
in order to be good enough?

Would you expect this from others?

No?

Then why put this pressure on yourself?

Chapter 1

HOW IT ALL STARTED

For the first nine years of my life, I grew up in a house in a cul-de-sac where lots of children played sports or British Bulldog in a nearby playing field. We all used to meet up after school or tea. There was always someone to hang out with and life was pretty good.

At primary school, I'd always been one half of a pair: I had one main best friend who I played with every day and I felt 'safe' in our friendship. Just before I started middle school, my friend decided to 'have other friends'. I wondered what I'd done and why she didn't like me anymore. I felt hugely rejected and didn't want other friends – I just wanted to go back to how it was. I got really upset and would blame it all on stomach aches and headaches.

Also during primary school, my mum had a nervous breakdown and suffered from agoraphobia and social phobia. She stopped doing everyday things like shopping and taking us out and I felt she became very over-protective.

Mum was very much the housewife, keeping our house immaculately clean, and Dad was the provider, working long hours and some weekends. I don't have lots of childhood memories but I do remember feeling loved, safe and secure, although there was a definite lack of affection from my dad, due to his own childhood. If I became upset, he would give me his 'magic hanky' rather than a hug, which was kind of cute but I also assumed it stood for: Stop crying, don't show your feelings.

I was always a fussy eater. My mum would cook the same thing each weekday, so you could always tell what day it was by the meal you were having. Two days of the week Mum would serve up a traditional English meal like potatoes, meat and vegetables with gravy, because that's what my dad liked (and he was fussy too so it was difficult for Mum). I hated these mealtimes; it felt like a battleground where Mum insisted I couldn't leave the table until I'd finished. I was determined I wasn't going to eat though and would sit there for hours. It was a total battle of wills.

When I reached my teenage years, I became quite rebellious and continually pushed the boundaries. I was 13 when I brought home my first boyfriend, an 18-year-old. My mum and I clashed all the time, and she would ignore me. At the time I was hurt, and felt that it was because she couldn't control me. It's only now I realise that my attitude stunk and she just wasn't buying into it.

I've always been small in size (I'm 4'11" now), which has constantly been an issue for me. I've been referred to as cute so much and treated as a 'sister type' by male friends, rather than being considered attractive like other female friends. I always felt that I was second best to them and my brother, too. I considered my brother to be the favourite due to his academic ability, his work ethic and his ability to toe the line. My parents always said that I could achieve just as much if I put in the effort. I didn't believe them, so I stopped trying and became even more rebellious. I ran away from the challenge for fear of failure. What if I actually tried my hardest and it wasn't good enough?

At 16 I left school with average GCSE grades and got a youth trainee position at a local engineering firm. It was a large company and I soon settled in, making many friends and enjoying a full social life. At the end of my training, I secured a permanent job in the marketing department.

At 19 I bought my first home, near to my parents and friends. I didn't have much money but I was happy and content with life.

At 21 I met Karl, an engineering student who was working with us during the summer holidays. After seeing each other for a few months, I decided to move to London to be with him and undertook a marketing degree. I was very motivated to study and was confident in terms of my work (even tutoring others), but, personally, I was deeply unhappy, as I'd lost my social network back home and the support of my family. I didn't have much money to go out socialising and didn't want to get into debt. I'd sold my house to ensure I didn't get into financial trouble. I felt there was a huge gap in my life and I was dependent on Karl. I started struggling with my confidence due to insecurities about my appearance and found it difficult to make friends. I lived with three other girls who I am still friends with now, but again I felt second best, as they were beautiful and popular, and I felt like the ugly duckling around them.

Soon after graduating, I returned home and started working with a local firm. I had my social life, friends and family back but soon decided to move to Scotland, again to be with Karl, as we'd struggled with our long-distance relationship. He had moved back to his childhood home in a rural village north of Inverness, ten miles from the nearest town. We rented our own place about eight hours' drive from my home. At first it was fine, as I soon started work that I enjoyed and I was busy, but then Karl's car broke down. My job stopped, and he started using my car for his work. We lived ten miles from the nearest town so I couldn't do any other work without use of a car and I felt 'trapped' in the house. In hindsight, I should have insisted he purchased another car...but I didn't. To try to combat this feeling of being trapped, I enrolled in distance learning, but I found this difficult as I wasn't used to studying alone by just reading books; it was boring and hard-going, even if it did fill my time. Yet again, due to my lack of confidence, I struggled to make new friends and became more and more lonely and isolated. Karl and I soon got engaged and I discovered I was pregnant. It was great news and we were excited, but I still spent most of my days trying to kill time and felt that there was so much missing from my life.

Whilst pregnant, I felt really ill and found that the only way of easing the nausea was to eat. Unfortunately, I literally ate for two, as I felt ravenous and hungry like

I had never before felt in my life. I just went with it, eating everything I fancied.

Of course I put on a lot of weight; in fact I'd put on four stone by the end of the pregnancy. We moved to Aberdeen shortly before the baby was due, and even though I didn't see many people, when I did I was embarrassed to be seen looking so huge. I wanted to tell everyone how small I usually was and explain that this wasn't the normal me.

After my daughter Erin was born I was still two-and-a-half stone 'overweight' and desperate to lose it. However, I had become used to unhealthy eating patterns and I really struggled. All my confidence and self-esteem was now gone due to being overweight, feeling lonely and being totally dependent on my husband. I didn't recognise myself; I felt like I'd become someone else. I used to be the life and soul of the party but now I struggled to make a conversation and I felt I had nothing of value to say. I'd control conversations by questioning people about themselves rather than talking about me.

Try not to compare yourself to others.

You are wearing filtered sunglasses and you will always look at yourself in the worst light, which will make you feel worse about yourself.

I can show you how to take the sunglasses off so you can see more clearly.

When Erin was one, we moved again, a few miles away. There was more of a feeling of community spirit and I made some friends and had a social life again. I also started to lose weight. I became pregnant and although I felt better, I still managed to put on a lot of weight. I had my second daughter, Jodi, but this time it wasn't such a shock to the system. I was happier and I started to lose the weight again.

But then we moved for the third time and I had to start all over once again. It's hard work relocating, and when you're not working, your main way to meet new people is at toddler groups, which I found rather boring. I'd been cooped up at home with my two young children all day and the last thing I wanted to do was sit with a load of women talking about their babies. Don't get me wrong, I love my girls desperately and enjoyed being their mother, but I needed something to inspire me as a grownup. However, I did make some good friends whom I was able to socialise with. I also became close friends with a woman around my age who, like me, lived far from her family and was struggling to settle. We spent a lot of time together and I felt more like my old self. I started to feel a sense of belonging. I was also more motivated to lose more weight (after losing quite a bit already) so I started on a calorie-controlled diet. I continued to lose weight and got to my target weight within three months. I was delighted.

Just when I started to feel settled and happier, my friend decided to go back to New Zealand to be with her family. Obviously I was happy for her but I was also gutted at the thought of losing her friendship. I was back to square one. I felt this was supposed to be an exciting time for Karl and me – newlyweds with a young family in a new place – but because I wasn't happy, I felt like a failure.

It was around this time that I had a bit of a health scare so we decided to move back to my hometown of Pershore. I was so happy and couldn't wait to be near family and friends again. Things were still difficult though, as Karl struggled to settle and I found that my friends' lives had moved on and I couldn't just pick up the life I had before I went away. I was a totally different person.

Karl worked away during the week and I struggled with the responsibility of taking care of our two daughters by myself. I felt that I couldn't cope with who I was, that I was still a child, still my mother's daughter – so how could I look after two children? I wanted to be a rebellious teenager again and craved the freedom that I once had.

I was eating little during the week while Karl was away at work and then indulging in food with him when he came home. I would lose weight during the week and put it all back on at the weekend.

I then decided to do an online accounting course, which I could do when the girls were in bed and while Karl was away. As I was so busy I lost more weight and quickly reached seven-and-a-half stone, which I've always thought of as my ideal weight – the weight I'd been before having children. But then, somehow, I became obsessed. I used to weigh myself every day and the dial on the scales would dictate whether I would feel happy or depressed that day, even though I never felt happy or content with my body, particularly my stomach or legs. I used to stand in front of the mirror and grab bits of fat and feel disgusted. I was convinced people were judging me on my weight and how I looked. I went through periods of crash dieting and bingeing and yo-yoed between seven-and-a-half and eight stone. I thought this was fine and perfectly normal.

About 18 months after moving back to Pershore, I found out that Karl was having an affair. I found emails on our computer and when I confronted him he seemed indifferent and certainly not remorseful. I asked him for details but he refused to give any. He moved out within 24 hours (telling me that he assumed that was what I wanted) and moved 450 miles away. I was devastated and my head was a mess; I was left with so many questions and tried to fill in the gaps. I threw myself into my new full-time job, working while the girls were at school and then at night after they'd gone to bed, and making sure my daughters were happy and healthy. I filed for divorce. My appetite dropped, as did my weight (to six stone ten), although I didn't feel this was an issue because I still ate and wasn't consciously restricting. I remember feeling such anger at Karl for going back to Aberdeen – eight hours away from the girls – to be with his girlfriend. I always tried to put the girls first and couldn't understand why he didn't. I also felt that we'd made the decision to have children together but now he'd decided he was bored of that game and so he left.

A few months later, I began a relationship with Chris and continued a pattern of crash dieting and bingeing again. In June 2007, I decided to diet again and seriously restricted my eating. At this time, I was working for an older guy who ran his own business. We worked together in an office and Chris became jealous. I was doing nothing to feel guilty about, yet I felt that I was in the wrong, I was bad and I was terrible, even though I didn't know why. Chris didn't trust me and I ended up not trusting my own thoughts. We split up in August, as I couldn't cope with it anymore; however, a few weeks later we got back together.

Don't feel good enough?

Write down the reasons and imagine trying to convince a judge with your 'evidence'.

Would your case be thrown out of court?

It was during this time that my battle with food really kicked in. My appetite had dropped again. I'd take my girls to school, go to work and then at the end of the day realise that I hadn't eaten anything. I wasn't worried about this, as my appetite dropping when I'm stressed is a usual pattern for me. At this time, I was eating a sandwich, an apple and a banana a day. I wasn't hungry though, so that was fine, and I was losing lots of weight.

People around me had started to notice my weight loss and were complimenting me. After a couple of weeks, I'd limited my eating again. I guess I couldn't control the issues in my personal life, so I focused on food and losing weight as I thought I *could* control this. Although I didn't think I wanted to lose more weight, I'd be delighted to see that I'd lost another pound the next day. I would still look in the mirror and see chubby legs and a hideous stomach.

I'd always had issues with my legs, probably because I'm, short and due to a comment made by a girl in my class at high school who told me that she wished she had legs like mine because hers were too skinny. I assumed she thought mine were fat.

I constantly compared myself to other women and would criticise myself for still being too big or not as successful as them. I convinced myself that everyone else had such wonderful lives.

After a while, I realised that it wasn't that I didn't want to eat but that I couldn't. I was now absolutely terrified that if I ate just one more calorie a day, I would put all the weight back on. I constantly thought about food and cooked lovely meals for my kids but never ate them myself. Social situations were terrifying too, as they always involved a meal, a piece of cake or something else to eat. I'd just sit and not eat anything, feeling everyone's eyes on me.

Life soon became a nightmare because although losing more weight made me feel happy initially, I was never happy with myself and wanted to lose more and look better when I looked in the mirror. I was also exhausted and freezing cold all the time. I will always remember an October half term when my girls were staying at their dad's house in Scotland and were due back the following day. I sat by a radiator in about five layers of clothing with my coat on and a huge duvet wrapped around me, just trying to get warm. I felt absolutely shattered, had no energy and was frozen, and I thought for a minute how pathetic and weak I must look. I couldn't take care of myself; how was I supposed to look after my girls when they got back the next day? I knew that I had to get better.

But it's one thing thinking that you want to get better and another actually seeking help, because in order to get better, you need to put on weight, which is the thing that terrifies you most. For me, there was an angel on one shoulder – my sensible side – telling me that I needed to eat to live and that I needed to get better, and a devil on the other telling me that if I got help, they'd make me eat and I'd get fat.

Luckily, my sensible side prevailed and I went to see my GP. I was so scared and took along notes that I'd made just in case my head went blank and I didn't know what to say. I was diagnosed with anorexia nervosa. I was completely shocked because in my mind I wasn't skinny and I was still eating, even if it was just an apple and banana most days. I thought that people with anorexia ate nothing or maybe just a piece of lettuce, and I still couldn't admit to myself that things were that bad. Even though a professional had put a name to it, I was in denial.

I was put on antidepressants, which made me feel like a zombie. I lost some hair and suffered with hot flushes. I hated them and stopped taking them as soon as possible.

My GP told me I needed to eat (great advice!) and I was referred to a counsellor. It took six months to get an appointment. During this time the constant battle in my head between the angel and devil continued, but I tried to be strong and I tried to eat.

It was difficult and I felt guilty and disgusting for eating, thinking of the scales the next morning. My dad told me not to stand on the scales, but I just couldn't stop: it was like I 'had' to. I really tried to be normal and eat, but eating just freaked me out and the pressure built up inside me. Food occupied my every thought. It was the first thing I thought about in the morning and the last thing I thought about before I fell asleep. I remember going to work one day knowing that when I got home I had a couple of hours free before the girls got back from school. I planned my first binge. I was terrified but excited at the thought of eating all the things I'd denied myself for so long and, although I knew I shouldn't, it was like something else had taken over me and I was no longer in control. I bought cakes, chocolates and other sweet stuff from various shops to hide the fact that I'd bought so much. I took it all back home and binged. I felt disgusting and so ashamed and terrified at the thought of what the scales would say in the morning. So I attempted to get rid of the food I'd just eaten. However, I still couldn't stop thinking of how I'd lost control and eaten loads and…oh no, the scales! I woke up at 2am, sweating with fear, so I went downstairs and did an hour-long intensive workout. I got up the next morning and, although I was petrified and didn't want to look, I was drawn to the scales as if I had no choice. I got on the scales. I hadn't put any weight on. I was ecstatic; in fact I felt as if I'd won the lottery. The relief, the joy!

*Don't think of recovery in terms
of how you will look.*

*This is irrelevant, even though
that's your focus just now.*

Recovery is about how you feel about yourself.

Recovery is about feeling good.

But then I remembered the feeling of being hungry and my body started screaming for more and more food. I wanted to eat as much food as I could get my hands on, I guess to make up for starving myself for so long. So then began my battle with bulimia.

I would go through cycles of starving myself and then bingeing and purging in secret. Social situations were terrible again, as I'd feel conscious of people watching to see if I'd eat. When I did, I'd feel them relax, but inside I'd be screaming. I'd eat little amounts to make others feel better but would feel disgusted with myself. This built-up pressure and anxiety would then drive me to binge when I was alone later on.

I suffered with bulimia for about a year, but eventually I threw my bathroom scales away so I wasn't in fear of them anymore. I fought every single day, several times a day, to change my behaviour. I'd make sure I had something going on all the time to distract me and stop me spending time on my own so I wouldn't be tempted to binge.

Things between Chris and I seemed better and we got engaged and planned our wedding. I felt he ticked all the boxes and was totally different to Karl, who never seemed interested in family time. Chris wanted to be with me and made me feel special, safe and secure.

I focused on the wedding and, as a result, I thought I'd slowly developed a normal way of eating and I didn't feel I was obsessed. But I was busy with the wedding – too busy to think about eating – and I soon realised I was back on the same path. I'd lost weight again and convinced myself that I just wasn't hungry, but I definitely didn't want to eat or put any weight back on.

Although I thought my eating and weight issues had relaxed, my underlying issues were still there and, as soon as the honeymoon was over, I became stressed again. Chris became jealous of my new boss. I started delivering workshops in schools on self-esteem, body image and eating disorders; I was helping people one to one and volunteering for eating disorder charities; and I studied counselling. Again, I was busy and my appetite went.

I started losing more weight. I had a list of 'safe' foods and 'bad' foods, and a 'safe' calorie allowance. Over time, as my illness progressed, the list of 'safe' foods became shorter, the list of 'bad' foods became longer and my calorie allowance reduced. I was in total denial though, until my granddad died and, as a result, I had a week of bulimic episodes. Bulimia is much more difficult to deny than anorexia. I decided I could no longer deliver the workshops in schools, as I realised I'd been preaching to young people about something I didn't adopt myself and I couldn't put on this 'act' any more.

I tried to talk to Chris about it but he didn't seem empathetic. I took him to see a lady who worked for an eating disorders charity so that she could explain my illness to him, as I thought he might listen to someone else. However, when we left the meeting he hardly acknowledged what she'd said and remained steadfast in his opinion. I gave him books to help him understand (as I'd purchased quite a few for my studies) but they remained stacked in the wardrobe, unread. I saw Chris as unsupportive. We had booked a few days away in Somerset (just the two of us) whilst the girls were visiting their dad, and I thought it would be good for us. It was nice, but eating out was torture. We did find a restaurant that had a menu that seemed 'safe' to me and I was able to choose something from it. Major achievement, I thought. So the next evening I wanted to go back to the same restaurant to feel 'safe' again; however, this lead to a big argument because Chris was then convinced that I fancied the waiter! I couldn't believe how much worse he made me feel.

I asked for help from my GP again, who said that I'd got better before so I could do it again and wouldn't refer me to a specialist at that time. I was gobsmacked and annoyed that I'd been turned away after working up the courage to seek help.

Things between Chris and I were getting really bad, as I continued to feel unsupported and felt angry at him. We had booked a week's holiday in the Isle of Wight but as the time approached I told Chris I wanted to go alone with the girls, as I didn't want to fight. He came anyway.

I remember the Isle of Wight being absolutely gorgeous with a Mediterranean feel, but that's one of the few positive recollections I have. The rest of my memories were of absolute torture. My girls love swimming and, being young, they needed adult supervision. So every day I'd take them down to the pool whilst Chris chilled out in the caravan. And every day I'd feel the pull to swim for an hour, which would have looked comical as the pool was a round shape with this feature in the middle and it was packed! I must have appeared mad swimming as fast as possible and trying to swim around everyone playing happily. And I had to do an hour plus another 20 minutes, because I'd obviously slowed down at some point. If my girls wanted to play during this time, I would say no – we'd play later. I'd barely eat anything during the day and then, in the evening, the girls would want to go for an ice-cream. Each day I'd say to myself that I'd earned an ice-cream: that I wouldn't put on weight due to the little food I'd consumed and the exercise I'd done, and before we left I'd thought that I would treat myself. However, when we were in the queue I'd stand looking at the options, and I'd feel the tears about to come because I knew I couldn't do it. I either went for the 'safe' Solero option or nothing at all. But then I'd binge on the food in the cupboards when the girls were in bed! Each morning I'd say to myself that I didn't need to get into the pool; I could just sit on the side and dangle my legs in the water. But no – once I was there, it was like something else took control of my mind and body and I didn't have a choice but to swim. Rational thinking was just not an option. After about five days of this, I explained to Chris how I felt tortured and asked if he could take them swimming one day – he said no. I also asked him if he could take the girls to get an ice-cream – again he said no.

Shortly after our return from this holiday, I started writing a diary.

Everyone has up and down days.

But you need the down days
to appreciate the ups.

When you have a down day, know
that it won't always be like this, and
just do your best to get through.

Be kind to yourself.

Chapter 2

BEFORE RESIDENTIAL

Friday 30th July

Food is constantly on my mind. I buy Chris a Chelsea bun to eat on Bredon Hill and when he offers me some, I can't take it. I'm dying to go to the café and think of indulging in cakes, etc. but know I won't be able to go through with it when I'm there.

I feel so guilty about eating in public. I'm all psyched up to eat and order but I can't! I always feel so guilty and want to binge after. It's just safer not to try.

Saturday 31st July

I feel like Shrek as my face is so fat. I'm not looking forward to seeing my uni friends as I don't feel confident. I arrived at Kay's and there were loads of nibbles on the table the whole time I was there. However, I didn't feel hungry so it didn't bother me too much and I didn't feel like eating anything. Later on I started to feel peckish and asked Kay for some fruit. She didn't have any and she told me what she did have; I couldn't choose and panicked over calorie content. I quickly grabbed a breadstick which was fine for me and I just wanted to stop them fussing. I was also offered bruschetta but I couldn't eat it as Kay had added olive oil.

Sunday 1st August

I woke up and wanted to go swimming. Well it was more like I felt the need to, so I did my obsessive hour plus slacking time.

After visiting Mum and Dad I had lunch – Weetabix (with boiling water), orange and yoghurt. It was raw veggies with chilli sauce for tea. Went to the gym for an hour's exercise. Went out to see a friend as a distraction but no real temptation. Phew.

Monday 2nd August

I felt hungry at work so had an apple mid-morning then Weetabix for lunch. I went to the gym afterwards even though it was a lovely day and I would've preferred to be outside but I'd paid my membership so I need to get value for money. I ate an orange before going. I did 50 minutes on the running and rowing machine plus ten minutes on weights. I had couscous and veggies for tea plus an orange, peach and yoghurt. Went for a walk in the evening.

I feel positive today. Is it because I'm not feeling really hungry and I feel in control?

Wednesday 4th August

I went to see Heather from the eating disorders charity and was very positive (I'm in control and losing weight). I told her about my coping strategies and tools like listening to music whilst shopping, starting to eat little bits during the day and trying to copy other people to see what's acceptable regarding food consumption. I met Nigel, Chris's brother, and bought three dresses from a shop. They each had a specific purpose, otherwise I couldn't have justified buying them. I ate dry Weetabix and a peach by the cathedral and had a good walk. We went for coffee and although I ordered an apple, I couldn't eat it so I took it home. The apple just looked huge and I wasn't particularly hungry anyway. I came back to Pershore determined to keep up my routine this week of going to the leisure centre, then shopping. I went to the gym for an hour – did 35 minutes of running, 20 minutes on the rowing machine and five minutes of abdominal weights. Went to the health suite afterwards as my reward. I always go to the gym thinking I'll just do half an hour of exercise but then the obsession takes over and I have to do an hour. Not 45 minutes, not 50 but the whole hour.

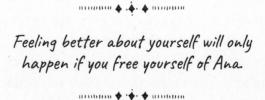

Feeling better about yourself will only happen if you free yourself of Ana.

Thursday 5th August

I feel tired and hungry today. Had my Weetabix at lunch. I feel the need to go and see Mum and Dad but I also feel the pull towards the gym. I'm not in the mood for exercise at all but the battle goes on in my head and I end up going for a swim for an hour then going to see Mum and Dad. I went to Number 8 to watch *Heartbreakers*, it was really good and very funny. I didn't think of food at all which is excellent.

Saturday 7th August

Had my normal dry Weetabix and apple for lunch. I had to weigh the apple as it was so big. Walked to supermarket and library but felt so tired; was like walking through mud.

〰️

OK – so things don't seem too bad, do they? I'm still eating at least and although I'm obviously having some issues, I'm still OK. Aren't I? Unfortunately, I am not, as it was around this time that everything went downhill drastically.

I eventually went to see another GP who referred me straight away to the eating disorders service but it was the summer holidays and staff were sick or on holiday. I had to wait three months for an appointment.

I saw my GP regularly and she tried to coax me to eat, offering advice and support, but I just sat, nodded, said all the right things and then went home and stuck to my plan, which was basically a Weetabix with boiling water for lunch and then my main meal of stir-fried vegetables (no oil though, of course, and I used a spicy, almost no-calorie sauce).

My relationship with Chris had reached a low point and I cut myself off from his family as he wouldn't try to explain my issues and feelings and I couldn't cope with the pressure of having to be OK.

Exercise had continued too, which increased when my girls were visiting their dad in Scotland. I'd be at work during the day and drive back absolutely shattered, saying to myself there was no way I was going to the gym or swimming, etc. But again I'd be drawn to the leisure centre and I'd do at least an hour of swimming or the gym, and then I'd have to do another 15 minutes in case I'd been slack at any point. I also got into running and would think nothing of getting out of bed and going for a six-mile run.

I was now at the stage where I felt as if I was sitting at the bottom of the deepest well, with not even a chink of light shining in. To me there was no hope of recovery. Every time I'd tried desperately to eat more, even the tiniest piece of food, I'd end up bingeing. This was far more terrifying than starving myself, so I decided that the safest option was to continue with my limited eating plan. I'd accepted that this is what I would do even if I did end up dying as a result. I felt as if I couldn't even make the slightest change to my diet and that there was no way out. I'd convinced myself that I was a total burden on everyone and that people (even my girls) would be much better off without me. Whilst I waited for an appointment, I lost another two stone and contemplated suicide every day.

In fact, one day I lined up so many pills in front of me because I had eaten more than I should and I was convinced that I was going to be huge as a result. I felt so tortured and just wanted it to end, and I thought that even if I wasn't successful in killing myself, at least they might pump my stomach so I could get rid of the food I'd just eaten. I got myself a glass of water and I was just about to start taking the tablets when my phone rang. It was my dad. I could have ignored the call and carried on, but to me it was a sign that I was supposed to keep going.

On another occasion, after eating too much, I considered drinking bleach or surgical spirit as a way of physically stopping myself from eating. I didn't think of the harm I could come to, of the physical damage I could do or of the pain that would come as a result; I just thought of it as a way to not eat in the future.

Feeling weak? Tired? Freezing cold?

Your central heating system needs fixing.

It needs fuel!

We were invited to Chris's niece's wedding in September. I was torn, as I desperately wanted to be part of her day but couldn't cope with the social and food aspects.

I decided to go to the church and then return in the evening when the meal was over. I have no recollection of looking skinny, although I do remember noticing all the bones jutting out of my back. I returned to the wedding to what would usually have been the best part, the dancing! However, I just sat in a chair feeling totally numb to everything that was going on around me, not even tapping my foot along to the music.

The day of my appointment finally arrived and I was terrified, but I knew I desperately needed help. I was immediately referred to the International Eating Disorders Centre in Aylesbury for residential treatment for four months. I had to go away for four months and leave my girls for that period of time. Chris was in France at the time and I texted him to let him know.

I was terrified of losing control, as I knew I would be made to eat there. But I also knew that I needed someone else to give me permission to eat so that if I did eat, although the voice would be telling me I'd failed, I wouldn't feel that it was my fault. I would be eating because someone else made me. Basically, someone else was fighting the voice in my head when I couldn't. It felt safer knowing that I wouldn't be able to binge when I felt guilty afterwards. I had a glimmer of hope; a small ray of light now shone down in the well. I also felt hope for Chris and myself – hope that if I became well again, our relationship would be better and our marriage would work.

If you felt good enough, had more confidence and self-esteem and felt more positive about yourself...could you tell Ana to go to hell?

Your eating disorder is not about your BMI. If you want help but aren't receiving it because you don't fit the criteria, look elsewhere! You deserve help just as much as anyone else!

Chapter 3

RESIDENTIAL (MONTH ONE)

Monday 13th September

I arrived feeling conflicted. Part of me was rather numb and empty of emotion, whilst another part felt a mixture of terror and relief. I was expected to eat Weetabix and milk for lunch and it was huge; there was just so much of it in that bowl and I felt full after only a couple of mouthfuls. I ate very slowly and did my usual habit of having just a small amount on a spoon. The size of the bowl and the spoon were huge too and it felt so unsafe. The health care assistant (HCA) encouraged me to put more on my spoon, which I did, but it just felt like so much food in my mouth. Eventually I finished after 40 minutes. It seemed never-ending.

Sylvia, the HCA, played the piano afterwards, which was really helpful and distracted me from what I had just eaten and how full my stomach felt. However, it only seemed like five minutes later that I had to go back upstairs for tea.

So I should explain about the Centre here in Aylesbury. At the moment, there are three ladies here other than me. Belinda on Level 1, Hermione on Level 2 and Angela in the flat on Level 4. There are various staff here today but apparently they tend to work different days so you have different staff more or less every day. They also use bank staff.

During the four months at Aylesbury you start at Level 1, where you cannot do anything except eat and talk. You are not allowed to go anywhere; you have to keep your bedroom door open at all times; and you can only use the toilets at certain times. Once you have progressed, achieved a BMI (body mass index) of 16 and read your autobiography (a brief background of your eating disorder) to the group, you can apply to be on Level 2. Applications are assessed at multi-disciplinary team (MDT) meetings. Level 2 brings privileges such as being able to go for a ten-minute supervised daily walk, going out for Skills Challenges and attending Cooking Skills sessions with Eric the chef. If you have continued to progress and achieved a BMI of 18, you can apply for Level 3, which means preparing your own teas and snacks, being able to shut your bedroom door at night, going for a ten-minute unsupervised walk and going home at weekends. The aim is then to spend a couple of weeks before discharge in the flat (Level 4) where you live more separately to other clients and live more independently, being in charge of all meals and snacks.

At meal and snack times, we have to go upstairs and wait outside the dining room before being called in by the HCA. Our meals are placed on the dining table with name labels on them and this is when you find out what you are eating. Wrappers are removed from all snacks so you cannot see how many calories they contain. We aren't allowed to talk about food at the dinner table or comment on our meal or anyone else's. This makes it really difficult if you have a concern that you want to raise.

Food will never hurt you as much as the voices in your head.

Eating healthily whilst enjoying treats is normal and balanced.

Meals are every day at:

- 8.30am: Breakfast

- 10.30am: Snack

- 1pm: Lunch

- 3.30pm: Snack

- 6pm: Tea

- 8.30pm: Snack.

That's a lot of eating! And it's exhausting! If that wasn't enough, we have other structured sessions each week:

Monday:

- 9.30am: Art Therapy

- 11am: Process Group (discussing the weekend)

- 2pm: Food Issues

- 4.30pm: Pilates

- Plus a one-to-one meeting with Sharon, psychologist.

Tuesday:

- 9.30am: Body Image

- 11am: Dietetics

- 2pm: Food Issues

- 2.30pm: Goal Setting

- 4pm: Roger's Pastoral Group.

- Plus a one-to-one meeting with Kathy, dietitian, and the psychiatrist.

Wednesday:

- 9.30am: Coping Skills

- 11am: Self-Acceptance

- 2pm: Food Issues

- 3.30pm: Skills Challenge

- 4.30pm: Roger's Pastoral Group.

Thursday:

- 9.30am: Family Issues

- 11am: Relational Effectiveness

- 2pm: Arts and Crafts

- 4.30pm: Roger's Pastoral Group.

Friday:

- 9.30am: Body Image

- 11am: Self-Acceptance

- 12pm: One-to-one with Sharon, psychologist.

Choosing breakfast was a nightmare as I didn't want milk or nuts. I wanted the safest option with the least amount of calories. I examined my tummy before bed. Very bloated! I'm scared. What if I've put on huge amounts already? Am I a fake to be in here? Got to get weighed in the morning!

They wouldn't let me have laxatives, which I was not happy about and felt like I wanted to scream. This will definitely affect the scales. I can see that once I feel physically stronger there may be a temptation to try to exercise if I continue to feel this full.

I feel weird about having to ask for everything – a glass of water, a hot-water bottle. They also do my washing and ironing for me!

꘎꘎꘎ꕢꕥꕢ꘎꘎꘎

Don't think of recovery as a long road.

It can be one day at a time, one morning at a time or even a few minutes at a time.

Tuesday 14th September

Went to the toilet and was weighed. Talked to HCA briefly about my fears about being weighed, the fact that I'd usually weigh myself naked and would've taken laxatives the night before. She tried to reassure me that others have the same fears and it becomes more routine and relaxed as time goes on.

Breakfast was two large crumpets with a lot of spread and a marmite sachet. Struggled with that and strawberry yoghurt for about 45 minutes.

Came down for group session on body image. We looked at our distorted thinking patterns. Wow, what a heavy session. Are you ready for what I found out about myself?

I am an all-or-nothing thinker:

- It's either total restriction or binge/purge.

- I need to be perfect in all roles otherwise I've completely failed.

- I'm always comparing my body to others', including teenagers', and I am a failure if I'm bigger.

- Exercise is either none or excessive (obsessive).

- I hate routine but thrive on it.

- I'm average and not special, I'm second best – so I'm a failure.

- If my relationship is imperfect, it's not going to work.

I catastrophize about:

- weight gain and seeing my body as fat

- if I start eating I won't be able to stop

- others seeing me as fat.

I jump to conclusions:

- I always feel that I must have done something wrong if someone is a bit 'off' with me.

- If someone says I'd like to talk, I assume it's bad and I've done something wrong or offended them.

- I always think people are looking at me and thinking I'm fat, ugly and wearing awful clothes.

- I always think people must be laughing and talking negatively about me.

- I'm too nervous to go into high-street shops as I feel shop assistants think I'm too ugly to shop there.

I do focus on the negatives:

- I focus on what I haven't done rather than what I have.

- I feel average in lots of things but special in nothing.

- I can have a whole conversation full of praise and positivity at work but I'll only remember the things I can improve on. I see this as failure and that I'm rubbish.

- I don't believe people when they say nice things about me.

I live by fixed rules and 'should' statements:

- I must be perfect in all my roles.

- I should know what my future career will be so I can plan for it, otherwise it'll be too late and I'd have wasted time.

- I must not eat more than 'X' calories per day to feel in control.

- I must do an hour of hard exercise.

- I need to feel successful.

- I must eat and prepare food in a certain way.

I label myself as:

- too big

- an ugly duckling

- not successful

- having done nothing to be proud of

- always failing

- having legs that are fat and stumpy

- having a stomach that is hideous

- having a face like Shrek's after I've eaten.

・・・・・・・ ◆ ・◆・ ◆ ・・・・・・・

*If you spend your life looking behind you
with regret, you'll miss what's around
you now and what's ahead of you.*

・・・・・・・ ◆ ・◆・ ◆ ・・・・・・・

Wow! If that wasn't hard enough to take in, at 10.30am it was time for a snack. I'm still full from breakfast! This is so hard and the HCA is telling me to keep an eye on the time. It took about 30 minutes to eat. Then it was monitoring.

Monitoring is when you all have to sit in the lounge after eating to make sure you don't try to exercise, make yourself sick, etc. The bathrooms are locked during these times too. And when you do get to go to the toilet, there is no lock on the door, only a laminated sign which you flip over for occupied or not occupied. And I'm not allowed to go out for a walk or anything. I can sit in the garden but I can't do anything active. Not even change my own bedclothes. I'm a mum who is used to doing everything; I can't just do nothing! I'm going crazy already.

Had a meeting with the dietitian. How much?! Seriously, she wants me to eat:

- Breakfast: two portions of carbohydrates (cereal/toast); one portion of fat (nuts/spread); one portion of dairy (yoghurt/milk) and dried fruit.

- Snack: small snack and fortified drink (called Ensure – tastes like crap and is full of calories!).

- Lunch: again, a mix of carbohydrates, fat, fruit/veg and protein, similar to today's meal.

- Snack: another one, only bigger this time.

- Tea: bit like lunch plus you have a dairy-style pudding with fruit.

- Snack: small snack and a milkshake.

Nobody can eat this much food in a day. This isn't balanced, it can't be. This must be food for all of us in here? Our last snack is at 8.30pm. I thought eating after a certain time was bad for you as your food doesn't have a chance to burn off? They're definitely trying to make me fat. Get me out of here.

For tea I had red and green peppers, hummus, chicken, half a wholemeal muffin, grapes and yoghurt. It took forever to eat, about 50 minutes. Totally stuffed but did actually enjoy the flavours. Feel really tired and head feels full of cold. Feel crap. Really intense day. Could kill for a Diet Coke but not allowed in here. Think I'm getting withdrawal symptoms.

Had difficulty choosing breakfast again so the HCA helped me with my choices. Thought I'd try a muffin as I enjoyed it today. I also wanted to try dried apple as I hadn't tried it before. Who am I kidding? I wanted to try dried apple as I thought it would have the fewest calories!

Wednesday 15th September

In Self-Acceptance with Tina, we talked about what we value in our life. What do I value? I don't seem to feel much at the moment and can't actually feel the value of a lot but I know from the past what I do value: trust; honesty; appreciation; kindness and consideration; good friendships and relationships; sense of belonging; feeling special; feeling safe and secure; confidence; feeling loved and needed; appearing strong; making a difference.

Have been feeling a bit lonely and I guess I had some time to think about where I was and the length of stay here. I was feeling upset that I couldn't see Chris at the weekend. Spoke to the girls and they were happy and enjoying extra attention from family and friends.

Got overwhelmed at tea as it seemed such a huge amount of food I had to eat. I was already feeling emotional and ended up crying at the table.

Talked to Joe (staff nurse) about my previous eating disorder workshops and he encouraged me to continue when I recover and said that I'd be a good advocate.

Thursday 16th September

I looked back at my childhood and how there was a distinct lack of affection with no real 'I love yous', few hugs and the magic hanky I would be given by my dad if I was upset. However, I do remember my dad tickling me on my knees with his chin on my chest and I would have to say 'I surrender' to get him to stop. I laughed so much it hurt.

I feel that my childhood and my divorce are at the root of my eating disorder. I need to learn from the past to try to see what's making me unhappy, what emotional issues I'm hiding from and what I need to fix for a brighter future.

‖‖‖‖‖‖‖ ◆ ·◆· ◆ ‖‖‖‖‖‖‖

If you want things to change, you need
to try doing something different.

‖‖‖‖‖‖‖ ◆ ·◆· ◆ ‖‖‖‖‖‖‖

At Food Issues group I asked Yota (support worker) if she thought I was a fake for being here. She was so lovely and said I needed to be there as much as anyone else. She explained that food would give me the energy to deal with my emotions; normal eating was occasionally missing a meal or occasionally overeating but not all the time. She told me that low-fat products weren't good for you as they aren't natural and your body doesn't recognise or acknowledge them so turns them into fat.

I had a chat with Roger, a local volunteer, who runs a pastoral group here; got upset when he talked about my girls and being away from them.

I found out my daughter Jodi is school councillor. I am so proud, she got five votes! I spoke to my girls today. They both sound really positive and happy.

Tea was really hard as there was loads of food and I was so full! It felt like my ribs were going to break under the pressure. It was chocolate trifle for pudding, which I was really anxious about as eating chocolate would usually be a trigger to binge. I also couldn't understand how chocolate trifle could be part of a healthy diet along with crisps at snack today; I definitely didn't feel good.

Friday 17th September

Got weighed this morning, which I was anxious about. Thought Cynthia (staff nurse) would gasp at how much weight I'd put on. In my session with Sharon I talked about my change in body shape and not having a little waist and good tummy. I spoke about my uncertainty about Hermione – she said in group today that she does not want to talk about food or feelings outside of group sessions. The thing is, the whole time we're here we are focusing on food and our feelings so what else have we got to talk about? I'm sorry I keep upsetting her but I'm new to this and don't know what the rules between 'inmates' are.

I talked in Food Issues group about my need to trust the staff. I'm not sure what normal eating is and I want to know that staff are going to teach me to eat properly but healthily and not give me rubbish and make me fat. I looked at my negative habits and routines that I had at home such as:

- drinking at least two litres of Diet Coke each day

- constantly chewing sugar-free gum

- weighing myself with all my clothing removed, after toilet, no food or drink, moving scales into exact position, pressing down twice and then stepping on and off twice to make sure dial is still at zero; then allowing myself to stand on and read weight, but then check the dial goes back to zero when I step off

- needing to eat exactly the same thing every day

- eating using the same bowl, plate, cutlery

- eating from the sides of the plate with small amount on the spoon or fork so it doesn't feel as much in my mouth

- taking a bit away from the edge of the plate to keep my food tidy in one pile

- cutting up raw vegetables in a certain way, in a certain order, into the tiniest portions, in exact amounts to make the meal last longer

- eating my yoghurt in a certain way, dipping my spoon in a couple of times and shaking off excess amount, then scraping around the edges of the pot so it's clean

- needing to tidy up before beginning my meal

- pulling pieces of food into small pieces

- eating slowly

- constantly checking calories and fat content

- needing to cook and have control of other family members' food

- not allowing Erin and Jodi to put their own sauce, etc. on their meals

- leaving the table straight after eating to clear others' plates and wash up

- putting the girls' treats in a particular cupboard so I don't see them – they are theirs and not for me

- obsessing about the girls' meals and snacks

- hating to waste food and needing to eat it just so it doesn't get thrown away

- opening one pack of biscuits or cereals, etc. and needing to finish this before opening another

- torture when having too many options – difficult to decide

- body checking in mirror.

꣠꣠꣠꣠ ◆ ·◆· ◆ ꣠꣠꣠꣠

Imagine yourself as an 80-year-old.

What would you regret?

Don't let this happen.

Make the change now.

꣠꣠꣠꣠ ◆ ·◆· ◆ ꣠꣠꣠꣠

Monday 20th September

Talked in Food Issues group about my need to know calories and I'm finding it really difficult not knowing in here. Yota encouraged me to think of portions rather than calories and said that when calories are labelled on foods in the supermarket, they are not usually accurate and can be up to 30% inaccurate!

As my body is getting bigger and I gain more energy, I am tempted to exercise even just to keep toned. It seems so unnatural to me to just sit around, as I never do this at home – I'm always busy and on the go.

Tuesday 21st September

I'm also feeling anxious about seeing Kathy, the dietitian today. Will she increase my meals? It will be tough as I'm already eating plenty. Or will she decrease my meals? That will show that I have put on lots of weight. Would I like her to continue as it is? Not sure.

Kathy didn't increase my meals (just kept it as it was), which apparently is normal practice. However, she will increase it to two portions of carbs at lunch and at tea next week. At least I have a week to try to work on the anxiety of that!

Went for a snack and had an elevenses bar but it looked smaller than usual so wondering if she has cut it down because I've put on too much weight. Tempted to exercise! Trousers getting tight!

In Goal Setting session today, my short-term goals for this week are:

- trust the staff here – that they know what they are doing, that they are here to make me healthy

- relax about getting bigger

- prepare for visitors this weekend
- finish my autobiography.

My medium-term goals are:

- prepare for weekends home
- learn coping mechanisms
- use more positive self-talk
- increase self-esteem
- review what I need to accept and what it would be best to change.

Long-term goals (post discharge):

- maintain healthy BMI
- continue hard work of recovery.

Received cards, letters and flowers today so felt pretty emotional, particularly after a hard day. Feeling very out of control and do not like my trousers getting tight. Aarrgh!

Wednesday 22nd September

I realised that usually as my weight goes up I dress more casual and drab, which reinforces a negative body image and doesn't help with my confidence. I need to start to dress more confidently even if I'm getting bigger.

I was pleasantly surprised at lunch as I don't normally enjoy boiled potatoes, broccoli, mangetout and cauliflower but as they were spicy, they tasted good. It took me a while to eat them but they were less heavy than the lasagne yesterday so it felt better. I need to challenge my thoughts of feeling guilty about eating and enjoying food.

I am applying for Level 2.

Thursday 23rd September

In group I said I struggled to communicate with my mum. She has done so much for me and I'm extremely grateful but I feel that I am not able to make decisions for myself as I place the expectation upon myself that I 'should' do things how she would want me to do them. I don't want to upset her but I need to stand up for myself; I also want her support. Communication with Chris is also tough – about practically anything, to be fair.

It was not your choice to have anorexia.

But it is your choice whether you want things to change.

I have been trying not to think about the food in front of me, counting calories, etc. and just trying to eat without thinking about anything. However, at tea, I felt really full – more than usual – so I started to question the amount in front of me. I had four quarter chicken tikka sandwiches instead of two. I whispered to Nicky (HCA), who was sat next to me, 'How many portions of carbs is one piece of bread?' She explained she couldn't talk about it at the table and that we'd talk after. After tea I went to my room and quickly checked my meal plan. For tea I am supposed to have one portion of carbs, one of protein, one of dairy, one of fruits and one fat. Joe tried to suggest I'd done wrong at the table and told me off for talking to other clients. He also maintained that it was my fault for not checking at the start whether my meal was right and for not mentioning it then. I should now just accept it. Julie (HCA) offered to change my evening snack to compensate but as I got double bread, surely I would have got double protein and fat too?

Saturday 25th September

Had night sweats for the last few nights; been having cramps in my legs and tonight my legs were a bit swollen.

Had a lovely afternoon today with Dave, Soph, Greg and Alex (my brother and his family). It was really relaxed and the kids weren't bored at all – in fact they didn't want to leave, which was lovely. Had a headache at the end of the visit though, perhaps due to anxiety. Really looking forward to seeing Chris and the girls tomorrow. It was great to speak to the girls on the phone tonight.

Monday 27th September

Feeling anxious about MDT meeting – will I get to Level 2?

Been here for two weeks now and it couldn't have gone much better really. I have been so lucky with food as there haven't been many things I've struggled to enjoy.

Need to speak to Rose (staff nurse) tomorrow about Level 2. Apparently it's a yes with conditions but she'll explain tomorrow.

Getting really irate at the dinner table with Kerry and Tracy (two new clients at the Centre) constantly saying they don't like things and wanting to change their meals. Mealtimes are chaos with everyone waiting downstairs and being called up 10–15 minutes late. Talked to Yota about this in Food Issues and she said I shouldn't let other people's anxieties at the table affect me – I need to cope better, distance myself, focus on my own eating and focus on my recovery not theirs. She told me that the journey to recovery is painful but the outcome is not.

She asked me for three examples of how I can affirm my self-worth through nurturing myself and eating. I would love to:

- allow myself to eat to be healthy without feeling greedy

- allow myself to enjoy meals and take pleasure in eating

- allow myself to let go of calories and trust in the angel side of me to challenge my devil side.

She also asked me for three examples of how I'm doing the maths (Yota's favourite phrase, which means providing evidence) to work out my feelings.

- I might have a BMI of 16 but this is still under-weight and I need to increase this if I want to be healthy and recover.

- My body is getting bigger but part of this will be muscle, which will be toned, not fat.

- I'm away from family and friends and not there to support them just now but in the long term I will be able to support them much more than I could do at the moment.

Tried on my other clothes this morning that Chris brought me at the weekend and felt better knowing that they were still too big for me.

Tuesday 28th September

Feeling like I'm doing too well here and I'm waiting to hit a wall. Maybe it'll happen if Kathy increases my meal plan. Anxious about calories again and want to know the number of calories in an Ensure although I'm sure it's about 400. I need to know what calories roughly I'm being given per day just to take the anxiety away. Asked Kathy if my weight gain is OK and I'm on target. Also asked if my meal plan will increase and then decrease and if I should be having 1500 calories per day.

iiiiiiiiiii ◆ ·◆· ◆ iiiiiiiiiii

*Just because you don't value yourself much,
it doesn't mean others don't. Never assume
what others think and feel about you.*

iiiiiiiiiii ◆ ·◆· ◆ iiiiiiiiiii

I know I asked her lots of questions but I just feel so anxious about my lack of control and not knowing what's happening and what the plan is. I'm worried that my weight gain will spiral out of control and they won't reduce my meal plan. Aarrgh!

In our Body Image session, I shared my frustration at not being able to exercise and how I wouldn't be toned. It was all very well eating, but I would just go all flabby and horrible rather than putting on weight nicely. Nice – what am I on about? Putting on weight definitely doesn't feel nice. But I need to, I know I need to. But I thought it was pretty much textbook stuff that you needed a good balance of food and exercise for your health! How will I cope when I leave here? How will I keep in control regarding eating and exercising? I guess the test will be the school playground and when real life kicks in again. What is it about the playground? I'm not sure but I do hate it. All these mums standing around waiting for their kids, chatting away, but to me it feels like judgement day. I think they're all looking at me, thinking I'm fat and ugly. I just want to run and hide and not be there at all.

I keep going over the BMI 16 calculation in my head to try to work out what weight I am: $2.25 \times 16 = 36$; $2.2 \times 36 = 79$. This means I'm now about five stone nine.

Felt achy during Pilates yesterday and was concerned that I'm not fit any more. Want to walk around. Have been getting cramps in my legs again, though, so maybe it's just tension. Realised I've become obsessed about my room and my bathroom routine. Everything has to be just so and in order.

Wednesday 29th September

I read my autobiography to the group this morning. I felt OK reading it but then felt very exposed and wondered if I had gone too deep and upset other clients.

At group we had to share how we evaluated ourselves. I evaluate myself by:

- how I look, such as shape, weight, legs

- success or failure

- how supportive I am to others

- how much time I give to others

- how confident I am

- how special I feel

- how in control I feel

- my ability to cope

- number of people in my life

- social life

- my job.

At Food Issues, Yota told me:

- be a woman, not a boy

- learn to love yourself

- everything you do for your children, do for yourself

- you need to invest in yourself emotionally as much as you invest financially.

As I'm now on Level 2, I went for my first Skills challenge. We went to Coffee Republic and my challenge was to order something other than a Diet Coke. Eating my snack away from the Centre felt strange but it was very relaxed and the conversation was good. I enjoyed my time out! I did feel disorientated not knowing where I was in Aylesbury and I wanted to study a map of the town centre. I guess as a way of gaining control? I also found being in WHSmith difficult as I felt bombarded by all the chocolates and sweets on display. I haven't felt that in a while. I just tried to blank it out. I also found it difficult walking through the shopping centre with all the mirrors and shop windows showing my reflection.

Thursday 30th September

Dying to do exercise as I feel so unfit and big. Thinking about food a lot and feel guilty about looking forward to eating. Trying really hard not to think about calories but really difficult, especially choosing breakfast and worrying about Ensure and the amount of biscuits I was given to eat today. Questioned Kathy again and also enquired as to why we have dried fruit rather than fresh fruit as fresh is supposed to be healthier and dried fruit is full of sugar, albeit natural. Apparently the dried fruit helps you go to the loo easier. Well that's one good thing but I'm sure I'd be happier with the fresh option. Kathy said that I have had no weight gain between 20th and 27th September. Whooppeee! Just as she gave me that piece of good news, she hit me with the fact that not only would my carbohydrates and fats be increasing as of now but puddings would probably start from next week! Pudding! I can barely cope with what I'm being given at the moment. Now, I know for definite that puddings aren't healthy. They're in the thinnest bit of the 'food-groups circle' chart – a place we're not supposed to go. Well, that's what Ana constantly tells me! Then, to brighten things up again she says that she'll soon be cutting down my Ensure (hallelujah!) but increasing my snacks. What? I feel like I'm on some kind of rollercoaster ride here and the problem is I can't get off, and every time I think I'm coming into the station, off we go again!

⚜ ⬩⬩⬩ ⚜

Just for today:
I will be kind to myself.
I will put myself first.
I will stop beating myself up.
I will do what's really right for me.
It's not selfish, it's crucial.

⬥ ⬩⬥⬩ ⬥

I feel tired today but the weather was brighter, so I spent some time outside. Went out for a walk with Ruth. Supposed to be allowed a ten-minute walk but I'm sure it was only about six. I wanted to have the full ten and felt disappointed. Was good to get out though.

Tracy said she ate well but her low weight was due to drugs. For a few seconds, I did think, 'Yes, that's what I can do so I can still eat.' What is the matter with me? Never going down that route!

Friday 1st October

In Body Image I talked about my nemeses – the scales and the mirror – and the need I had to keep checking both to stay in control. Only I always hated what I saw in front of me; I was never happy and always needed to go further. I remember the way I used to measure myself on the scales, stepping on and off to make sure that the dial went back to zero exactly before I finally got on. And then I would have to do it all again, just in case.

So relieved at morning snack to find a pear was waiting for me. I love fresh fruit and really missed it.

In group I shared that I felt OK and positive but I still struggle at times during the day. I feel tired. I also feel guilty about doing OK. This is the first time I've put myself first and I feel selfish.

Saturday 2nd October

I felt a bit faint today and went giddy and had a headache when I got up from sitting. The staff took my blood pressure and pulse. BP was 90/49 and pulse was 88. Felt really hot and weak and couldn't stop shaking. Just rested though and felt better later on.

So good to get out for a drive with Jan (HCA) today and the lake was gorgeous. I really wanted to walk all the way around but knew there was no way they would let me.

Up until now I've been writing down the times it has taken me to eat meals and snacks. I've decided to stop doing this so I don't focus on it too much and I hope I'll be more natural in my eating speed. However, as my lunch and tea have been increased in terms of size, it's definitely taking longer. Is this why I don't want to write it down, because I think I'm going back a step or failing?

Sunday 3rd October

Excited about seeing Chris and the kids this morning. Can't decide what to wear – the dress that Chris bought me for my birthday is pretty but makes me look big. Will try some stuff on after my shower. I eventually decided to wear the dress but with a belt. Although it looked a bit weird, I also looked smaller in it.

Great visit from girls and Chris but it went so quickly.

Disappointed to get beans on toast today. To me it's a childhood meal and I much prefer other meals I've been trying here. The amount of margarine still feels like a crazy amount and I hate it. The Ensure given was warm (not cold) and tasted rank, not that it tastes particularly good anyway. Had to eat a stick of cheese today, which was really difficult as I'm not much of a fan of cheese and haven't eaten it for ages, particularly knowing the fat content it has. I used positive self-talk and relaxation methods to manage my emotions.

Rested a lot today as I am still feeling a bit giddy – is it due to the antidepressants? Feel a bit jittery at times too. Am still getting night sweats and my hair is falling out again.

Monday 4th October

No night sweats last night but I felt nauseous. Need to check side effects of the antidepressants.

Talked to Rose about a possible trip to the theatre, and I am allowed to take the girls to the park this weekend if no exercise is involved.

Talked to Rose and Joe about applying for Level 3 as I am progressing well. I am not feeling guilty about eating and enjoying food anymore. I've faced my biggest fear – chocolate – and although it was difficult I was able to talk myself through it. I see being here as my only way out of this eating disorder: I couldn't do it on my own; I feel safe here; I've been given a great opportunity. I now have hope for the future and I'm going to give it my best shot. I feel relatively safe but now need to challenge myself to go further.

Did I really just say I'm not feeling guilty about eating? Well not as much as before anyway.

iniiiiiiii ♦ .♦. ♦ iiiiiiiin

*An eating disorder is a label for your
current condition so that doctors
can diagnose and treat you.*

*But the label can be temporary and can be
removed whenever you're ready to take it off.*

iniiiiiiii ♦ ·♦· ♦ iiiiiiiin

Tuesday 5th October

I told Kathy that I was feeling a bit more relaxed about calories and eating chocolate here. I have now eaten chocolate a couple of times and am feeling less guilty and safer knowing I can't binge afterwards. In the next breath she tells me she's increasing my juice and Nesquik by 50ml, two of my snacks are being increased and I'm getting puddings on Friday. I'm going to keep my mouth shut next time.

We have a discussion with Kathy about women in magazines with positive attitudes towards food. Well, I'm not sure about this as the only women featured in gossip magazines are being criticised for either being too skinny or too overweight. I hate magazines. You can't win.

She also asked us for five breakfast ideas, lunch ideas and evening meal ideas. I really struggled with this and even though I knew I wouldn't have to make or eat it, I felt quite anxious as I started to think about it. Eventually I came up with these.

Breakfast ideas:

- boiled egg with toast, grilled tomatoes/ mushrooms, fruit salad and yoghurt

- toasted teacake and fruit smoothie

- muesli with milk and fresh fruit

- crumpet with Marmite, fruit juice and yoghurt

- bagel with salmon, cream cheese and dried fruit.

Actually I lied: I didn't suggest these at all; well I did the muesli one but the other ones just sound too much. I feel full up just thinking about them! But I did come up the next lot.

Lunch ideas (each plus fruit):

- tuna salad with sweetcorn

- pitta bread with chicken salad and hummus

- ham toastie with salsa

- bean salad in wrap

- lentil and coriander soup with croutons.

Evening meal ideas:

- chicken fajitas

- kedgeree

- stir-fry with noodles

- spaghetti bolognese

- chili con carne and couscous

- risotto with roasted Mediterranean vegetables.

Wednesday 6th October

Had group session with Adele, family worker. We talked about the difficulty in making choices; how 'what ifs' weren't allowed as they are wasted energy; the need to not take things personally.

Saw Dr Kindell, the GP who visits here – the staff weren't happy that I was taking four laxatives a day so he reduced the dosage to three ☹ Don't think he's here next week though, so I know I've got at least a month more of taking at least some laxatives.

Really struggled at tea – feta cheese was awful and tasted like sick! And the salad was just carrot, beetroot and celery. Horrible. Felt really angry that I was made to eat the cheese, hating it and knowing it was full of calories and fat. What a waste of calories! Felt tempted to make myself sick, self-harm or do some serious exercise. Glad I had bananas and custard to end with, but I was really full.

ıı ıı ıı ıı ıı ◆ ·◆· ◆ ıı ıı ıı ıı ıı

*Want to feel loved? Special? Like
you belong? Good enough?*

You are!

*You're just looking at your life
from the wrong angle.*

Stop focusing on the negatives.

Start seeing the positives.

They are there.

You just won't let yourself see them right now.

ıı ıı ıı ıı ıı ◆ ·◆· ◆ ıı ıı ıı ıı ıı

Thursday 7th October

In group I talked about Chris eating lots of snacks and opening lots of varieties of food at once, and how it terrified me because once something is open, I then feel the need to eat it so it's out of the way and not wasted. Rationally, there is so much waste in the world and my little bit will not make too much of an impact but, still, I hate it! The other thing I find terrifying is buffets and social eating functions. I just shake in fear because all I see and think of is the food in front of me and it pulls me towards it. I usually start by not eating anything at all but once I let myself have a little something, that's it. It's like the dam has just broken and I'll binge.

Sun was shining today – lovely and looks set to be good weather for a few days. I love the sun and it makes such a difference to how I feel.

Friday 8th October

In Body Image today I talked about wanting to feel confident in nicer clothes but that I couldn't wear them as they were too nice for me: they would be wasted on me and I didn't deserve them. I also didn't want to stand out and wanted to blend in.

I enjoyed my apple and melon today. Fresh fruit!

We had a relaxation session with Adele, which I really enjoyed as I'm used to meditation but the other clients here hated it and caused such a fuss I ended up wishing we hadn't bothered.

Saturday 9th October

Had a great afternoon with Chris and the girls at the park and in town. It went so fast though. I felt tired afterwards.

Sunday 10th October

Tired again this morning and fell asleep after breakfast. Dave, Soph (brother and sister-in-law) and Dad came at 11.30am and we went to Watermead. It was lovely and the weather was nice. Had a little walk by the lake. Dad was looking at me and I knew I'd put on weight so I warned him not to comment, just in case, as my dad is as subtle as a sledgehammer. Mum sent me a lovely letter but I felt bad as I would've normally cried when I read it, but I just can't really cry at the moment and that makes me feel guilty.

Came back for lunch then we sat in the garden and chatted. Sad to see Dad go.

Monday 11th October

Worried about trying other clothes on. Want them to still be really loose. Not going to happen though, as I know I need to get bigger, but I don't like it.

I talked in Food Issues about having three chocolate cereal bars for evening snack in the last four days and other cereal bars and chocolate biscuits. It's just not right to be eating like this. I thought we were supposed to be getting a variety and food that was healthy. Everyone knows that cereal bars are just crammed full of sugar. Are the staff just too lazy to prepare anything else? When I asked why we have similar snacks each day, I was told it's because of the number of bank staff the Centre uses. A food diary was recorded but I guess some bank staff don't read it, or they choose to ignore it and grab something convenient.

Tuesday 12th October

Kathy asked me what my target weight was. What a stupid question. I wanted to say. 'As low as you'll let me get away with.' I knew this wasn't the answer she was looking for, but come on. The only consolation is that I might make it to Level 3.

〰〰〰 ◆ ·◆· ◆ 〰〰〰

On your darkest days, search for
any chink of light and focus on
that to help you through.

〰〰〰 ◆ ·◆· ◆ 〰〰〰

Our group session with Kathy involved going over meal plans. Our meals need to have variety, have balance and be easy to cook, and our fruit and vegetables should be the colours of the rainbow. Each day we need:

- three portions of dairy

- two to three snacks

- three portions of wholegrain products

- five portions of fruit and vegetables.

I know I should be getting used to this by now but it seems such a lot of food for one person in one day. She then asked us – just to make me feel really guilty and put my anxiety through the roof – for ideas for puddings and snacks. This is what I came up with.

Puddings:

- summer fruits and yoghurt

- raspberries and meringue nest

- fruit salad and custard

- bananas, chopped nuts and ice-cream.

Snacks:

- malt loaf

- fruit

- chopped vegetables or breadsticks and salsa

- nuts.

The above seem a bit safe to me but then again I've become the queen of knowledge when it comes to losing weight so anything else seems totally alien. I've still got no idea what 'normal' is.

Always people pleasing? You are
just as important and more so.
Make sure you are happy too!

What positive qualities does your
best friend love about you?

I bet it's not about what you
look like or what you weigh.

Do you choose friends based
on looks and weight?

Why is it so important for you then?

Chapter 4

RESIDENTIAL (MONTH TWO)

Friday 15th October

In group we talked about good qualities that we have and how we should place value on these rather than what we look like, what we weigh, etc. – qualities such as being kind, supportive, good listeners and funny.

Sunday 17th October

Had a great day with my friend Claire who came to visit today. Claire is so busy with her kids yet she is the one friend who has come to visit. She has also been helping with my girls at home and has sent me flowers! Feel overwhelmed and very privileged to have her as a friend.

Monday 18th October

Felt light-headed and weak (my blood sugar is low) this morning because our snack was moved to 11am.

How can I be hungry whilst eating so much? I hated feeling hungry, it made me feel scared.

Wednesday 20th October

A few people are going to support me going to Level 3! Whoop whoop!

In our group session today I talked about the label of having an eating disorder. The thing is, I don't want the label if I'm OK but if I'm struggling I don't want people to think I'm sorted just because I'm eating again and just because I've left here. If I'm struggling I need to write down my thoughts and feelings and use positive self-talk and the best-friend approach (talk to myself as I would talk to my best friend). I know I was always reluctant to ask for help before, as I wanted to retain control and prove I could do it all and I could succeed, but where did that get me? In here, that's where!

Saturday 23rd October

Was able to go out with Chris this afternoon from 2pm until 6pm and then 7pm until 11pm. We went into town for a drink and walked around the shops. In the evening we went to see *The Social Network* at the cinema. It felt really strange, though, having to go back to the Centre and him going to the B&B. Felt like we were little kids, not being able to spend the night together.

Sunday 24th October

I went through Level 3 forms with Clifford (staff nurse) this morning. He's feeling confident and is supporting me, so fingers crossed.

⋅⋅⋅⋅⋅⋅⋅⋅⋅ ◆ ⋅◆⋅ ◆ ⋅⋅⋅⋅⋅⋅⋅⋅⋅

People learn by example. If we're constantly beating ourselves up and putting ourselves down, why are we continually surprised when others do it to us too?

⋅⋅⋅⋅⋅⋅⋅⋅⋅ ◆ ⋅◆⋅ ◆ ⋅⋅⋅⋅⋅⋅⋅⋅⋅

Went out with Chris again during the day between 10am and 4.30pm. We went to Coombe Hill, had lunch in Wendover and then went to Wendover Woods and Tring Reservoirs. Felt so free, and felt normal being able to spend time with my husband. Lovely to spend time outside in the fresh air.

Monday 25th October

I've had a headache today and struggled to keep my eyes open so had a lie down between 12.30pm and 1pm.

It's the MDT meeting today, and this time my Level 3 application will be discussed. I felt so nervous and excited. Not sure how it'll go as it's quite rare for someone to be on Level 3 so soon. Rose is worried I'm trying to be the perfect client and complying because I'm trying to please everyone to get a hypothetical 'A grade'. She is probably right.

Had my first Cooking Skills session today. I was a bit worried about this as I'm no cook but I was surprised at how well I got on and Eric (the chef) was really pleased.

I talked with Sharon about my weekend with Chris and in particular his insecurities about our relationship. He's convinced I'm going to run off with someone else and is also worried about how I'm going to turn out after I go back home following this programme.

I got Level 3! I went on my first unsupervised walk!

Tuesday 26th October

It was really fun in Body Image today (*not!*), as we had to fill in a sheet and make a note of when we had a negative thought or feeling about our body image. Well that's the whole day really, then, isn't it? So are you ready for it? This is my day of feeling crap:

At around 8am when I wake up I feel big. I am lying down and the first thing I do is touch my tummy, check my stomach and tops of legs to see how big they are. I then go and sit down on a chair to check the size of my legs when they are against the seat of the chair. I constantly check my legs when I'm stood up or sat down.

When I see someone thin on TV, I feel huge. I immediately compare myself to them. I constantly check my stomach, whether I'm stood up or sat down. I check how my clothes fit and compare it to when I wore them previously. I check how my clothes feel as the day goes on. I avoid looking at my body at the end of the day as I know I'm bloated and fat, so I quickly change into my pyjamas. I check my face for bloating in the morning and every time I wash my hands. I check my reflection in the shower, book cabinet, upstairs fire door, conservatory – everywhere there's a reflection really. I check my arms for veins and I check my back for bones.

Why do I check myself so much? I'm trying to find out how big I am. I'm looking for reassurance, which only happens occasionally. Checking myself is so automatic, as I feel fat a lot. I know it takes up a lot of my head space and is probably not healthy.

Had to see Yota to discuss Level 3 and do an induction, as there's a lot of changes now and more responsibility involved.

As I'm now on Level 3 I am making my own teas and preparing my own snacks. Again, it's exciting yet scary. I feel more in control but it's difficult making decisions and it's tempting to keep to 'safe' foods. I've come this far though. I need to keep going; I can't go back.

Told Kathy that I don't want to know my weight. When you're on Level 3 you can look at the scales and discuss your weight with staff but I've decided against it. It was a really hard decision to make and I'm still not sure it's the right one. I'm so tempted to find out. Thing is, I've been so obsessed with my weight that I need to start letting it go. I'm going to be heavier and I'm not going to like it, so why torture myself? I need to focus on being healthy – that's why I'm here. Blooming hard though!

My short-terms goals for this week are to:

- continue to be positive and to challenge any negatives

- check out and sort volunteering opportunities whilst I'm here and think about future work

- relax and not think about calories when choosing snacks and meals.

Wednesday 27th October

In group I talked again about how guilty I felt that I was feeling positive and happy. Everyone else seems to be struggling far more than me and, although I'm struggling, I'm determined to get better. I feel guilty because of my success so far and am worried for the others. I did say that I'm worried about leaving though and that people may think I am sorted, but I shouldn't use my eating disorder as a cry for help and I should just talk more openly about how I'm feeling.

Real recovery is not about weight, eating or food etc.

It involves changing our mindset.

Thursday 28th October

I challenged myself to have Nutella at breakfast and really regretting it now. I feel like a teenager who rebelled, only now I'm worrying about the consequences. At least I know I am safe though and won't be able to binge.

I'm also looking into buses and trains that will take me back to Pershore as now I'm on Level 3 I also get to go home for weekends!

Need to do some meal idea sheets so I can plan what to cook now I'm on Level 3. I hate cooking.

Friday 29th October

In Body Image today we talked about the negatives of my body getting bigger. Well I could be here all day really, but seriously, I thought I would feel stronger but I felt stronger when I exercised hard and I could run, etc. I feel more tired now. Actually no, I feel exhausted now. How does that work? I guess the positives are that my dizziness and the brain freeze have gone. I think my mind is more positive – I can actually think more rationally now rather than being like a zombie and just going through the motions of life.

Felt anxious and unsettled at tea as I wasn't sure what to have! I hate making choices!

Saturday 30th October

I cried when I saw traditional-style meat, potatoes and vegetables with gravy for lunch, which is my worst nightmare. I find it bland and boring and when I saw it on my plate I just lost it.

Sunday 31st October

Had a dream last night that I was at Mum and Dad's house eating Sunday lunch and I forgot to count portion sizes. I got so scared in the dream and woke up feeling anxious – it was horrible.

Monday 1st November

In Process Group I talked about not being able to cry. Not that I want to be a crybaby or anything but a few well-placed tears wouldn't go amiss. I'm usually so sensitive and it seems strange – I feel cold and heartless because of not being able to show my emotions.

In Food Issues, Yota said Sharon had commented that I looked much younger. Yota said that now when she talked to me I was interesting. It's nice but I feel a bit embarrassed and want to hide away.

Had my one-to-one with Sharon and I confided in her that, before, I'd struggled to recognise the difference between skin and fat. I'd grab hold of my skin and be convinced that it was fat. I'd feel disgusted when I looked at it and need to restrict my eating further and work out more to get rid of it. I'd been working so hard already – how could that fat still be there? I realise now that although my body (including my muscles) had shrunk, the skin around it had not, and I was left with excess skin, which I'd just viewed as fat.

Thursday 4th November

Had to do my risk lunch today. That's where I have to go out to a restaurant and order and eat a meal. Sound easy? I actually didn't feel too scared, which shows I've come a long way, and I went with Yota so felt safe with her. At first we were going to an Indian restaurant but it was closed so we went to the Plough pub near Bedgrove. We sat down and discussed my options, what I liked, etc. I was concerned about portion sizes and wanted to order the right portion. I also battled between what I fancied and the safe options. Yota explained that I should order what I wanted and just have in my head what the correct portion is and eat that. That was reassuring and I felt more relaxed. It also felt strange being told by a member of staff that I could leave food on my plate, as this is not allowed at the Centre.

I was going to order a veggie option but Yota said that I shouldn't due to the protein content. I eventually settled on piri-piri chicken, chips and salad. I was tempted to order a jacket potato instead of chips as a healthier option. However, I knew I wanted the chips as I love them and would always eat too many at a restaurant so this would be a good test. I was really relieved when the meal came because it wasn't huge and wasn't covered in oil or sauces. It felt OK. I was able to eat most of it but ate to a sufficiently full feeling and was able to leave some chips, not because of calories or anorexic feelings but because I was nicely full. I did initially get anxious about the salad dressing but I quickly accepted that I needed fat in my meal. I was able to have a normal conversation with Yota which was really nice and again felt more normal, as at the Centre the conversation can be quite stilted and awkward, particularly if the clients are having a tough day and feeling emotional. It affects everyone else. You try not to let it affect your recovery but it's very difficult.

When I felt really full, I told Yota, and she gave me permission to stop eating. She told me that you are allowed to eat till you're full and then, if you want to leave the rest, you can. But when you have been starving yourself for so long, you can feel full after a mouthful of food, or otherwise that mouthful can trigger a binge and you feel like you could eat a horse (not literally, obviously!). I think I'm finally beginning to realise and understand what 'normal eating' really is.

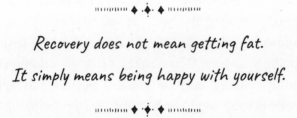

Recovery does not mean getting fat.

It simply means being happy with yourself.

Friday 5th November

Erin has a class assembly today so feeling a little upset that I can't be there this morning but one big consolation is that I get to go home today. So excited!

As it's the family tradition, we went to Dave and Soph's for a bonfire and sparklers. I recalled the previous year when I didn't eat a thing and felt tortured by the food Soph had cooked but tonight I was able to eat what

I thought was the correct amount and didn't feel guilty. No bingeing for me. Whoop whoop!

Saturday 6th November

I didn't sleep well last night.

Took the girls to their swimming lesson, which was lovely as I haven't done this for a while and it was great to see them swimming and to see how much they have improved, but – damn! – I forgot about the early start.

Was a bit anxious at breakfast. Felt so weird measuring out everything at home and I was on edge and tense the whole time.

Had Mum and Dad, Dave and Soph and the kids around for lunch. It was a bit scary and I felt anxious in the kitchen but more relaxed than breakfast, as there was no measuring involved – it was only lunch and just a sandwich. I managed to get through it OK without snapping at anyone. That makes a change. I don't mean it but if someone asks me a question when I'm feeling panicky getting food ready I just end up snapping the answer. I have no idea that I am about to snap, it just comes out and it leaves me feeling guilty. No guilt today though.

Met up with Rachel, Marina, Sandi, Auriol and kids (friends from Pershore) this afternoon in Wacky Warehouse. Was excellent to see them and although I gave them the lowdown on what life at the Centre was like, we didn't talk about this for the whole afternoon. We talked about what was happening with them and we had a good laugh. I felt part of the conversation rather than just watching them, as I've done before because I had nothing to say. I was even relaxed about the girls having chocolate, although admittedly I controlled how much they had.

Claire took the girls to a fireworks display this evening so I was able to spend some time alone with Chris. We went out for dinner and I was able to portion out my meal and leave the rest. It felt great and was a big achievement. I even felt comfortable with Claire offering the girls sweets when I picked them up.

Sunday 7th November

Went to see both my nans this morning, which was really nice. I'm now allowed to use email, and they said how much they're enjoying my emails each week (my dad prints them out a copy) and knowing how I'm getting on.

Went to see Sue, Chris's sister, this afternoon, which was lovely as we saw a lot of his family, but I felt really nervous about seeing them for the first time in ages. However, I did manage to relax and enjoy the conversation. I didn't worry about the girls having cake, and I had a chocolate biscuit even though I had already eaten my snack. So chuffed with myself, and I didn't do any exercise!

Monday 8th November

I told everyone about my successful weekend!

But...I can't believe it. I lost weight this weekend so I'm not able to go home next weekend! I spoke to Chris to tell him and he's not happy with me and said I must have gone back to my old ways and deliberately not eaten enough. Spoke to Mum and Dad, who said I'd been far more active so this was probably the reason. Even so, I feel crap. I talked to Sharon about this and the issues between us and she advised me to ask Chris to think of what issues he feels he needs to bring up during family therapy. I asked him but I can tell he doesn't want to come; he will, but he thinks it's a waste of time and that it's all my problem.

Recovery is taking one bite at a time.

Tuesday 9th November

Apparently I lost half a kilo at the weekend so I now need to wait until the weekend of Jodi's birthday, which is two weeks away, before I can go home for another visit. I'm allowed free rein during this weekend and can go home for the day on Saturday. I phoned Chris and he wasn't happy – he said extra activity wouldn't have made that much difference and suggested I must have cheated or not eaten enough. He said I had to find out what went wrong so it doesn't happen again. He also asked what had happened to my weight Monday to Friday. This made me feel crap, as if I was being accused and interrogated.

I really tried this weekend and keep wracking my brains trying to be honest with myself as to whether I did eat less than I should have. I honestly don't think I did. It's like working your butt off for an exam only to fail anyway and then be told by someone, 'Well I told you if you didn't study you wouldn't pass!' I feel so disappointed.

I spoke to staff about my loss of weight and they said that it is quite normal.

Wednesday 10th November

Spoke to Adele. She said the decision regarding the weekend was not because I'd lost weight but because I'd had a full-on weekend and I needed time to reflect, relax and assimilate so I don't do too much too soon.

You have survived so much already
with your eating disorder.

You are strong enough to do recovery.

We wouldn't wish anorexia
on our worst enemy.

So why do we think it's OK for us?

Chapter 5

RESIDENTIAL (MONTH THREE)

Monday 15th November

I'm feeling pretty pleased with myself that I've got to Level 3, although Rose is convinced I'm treating being here as a job and she fears that I'm giving it 100% now but it won't last once I get back out and the job's over. I can kind of see where she is coming from as I am giving it 100% because I'm very appreciative of being given this opportunity, although it's flipping hard work and I probably don't seem very appreciative at times (because I'm not). So I am at Level 3 and I am pleased but now I am struggling because I am thinking that it is enough – no more weight – I need to maintain it now and I'm scared. I've always struggled with maintaining weight in the past – it either goes down or up but never really the same.

I am also struggling with the talk in here about doing exercise. It's a well-known fact that one of the newer clients, Jasmine, is exercising in secret in her room and another, Bella, is talking a lot about self-harm and threatens to use her razor that she has stashed in her room. Talk like that doesn't help, as you have your own stuff to deal with and, although I instinctively want to help these people, I'm finding myself letting go so that I can concentrate on my own recovery. I really don't want to be pulled back into these girls' mentalities. I sometimes feel like I'm winning this; I just don't want to jeopardise it.

Wednesday 17th November

I had my first session at The Oaks today and really enjoyed it. The Oaks is a café/shop and is really busy so you don't get bored. I learned how to serve filter coffee, espresso, cappuccino and hot chocolate. It's actually quite tricky though, so I am not feeling that confident about that bit. I was much happier serving customers and using the till. I also got to stock the shelves and wash up. Sounds boring but it gives me a variety of things to do.

Friday 19th November

I talked to Sharon today about my weight plan and was looking for reassurance that my current meal plan was OK to maintain my weight and that I wouldn't put on any more. It's really freaking me out, as is my changing body shape. I know it needs to happen in order to get better but I don't have to like it. Well, maybe I do but... aarrgh! Get me out of here! I've always compared myself to other females in terms of weight – even teenage girls

– and if they look smaller than me I punish myself by working out extra hard or eating even less, because I feel like a failure for being bigger. I don't want to be normal weight, I don't want to be normal: I want to be special. Anorexia always made me feel special.

Went home for the weekend.

ıııı'ıı ◆ ·◆· ◆ ıııı'ıı

The only person stopping you from feeling happy and good enough is you!

ıııı'ıı ◆ ·◆· ◆ ıııı'ıı

Tuesday 23rd November

I discussed trying for Level 4 with Sharon. I am whizzing through this programme and feel really pleased but again there is a compulsion to be the star student, to please everyone and do the right thing. I have come so far so quickly; I am not going to throw this away when I get out. I am feeling scared about leaving here though. It's a strange feeling because I came in and felt like a prisoner because I wasn't able to do anything, but now it feels frightening thinking about going back out there into the scary world and facing everyone and everything again. One thing I can't get my head around is going back to my job; I just can't handle that. It is almost as if I would be going back and just carrying on as if nothing ever happened, that I hadn't been away for four months. I think I have come to the decision that I need to resign in order to feel calmer about leaving here. I feel bad for David and Claire (my bosses) because they've been really good to me and really supportive, but ultimately I need to put myself first and it is what feels right for me. I need to do it now though, so I'm giving them ample notice; I don't want to just spring it on them when I leave in January. Not sure what else I'll do but I guess I can figure that out another day.

Thursday 25th November

Sharon asked about my discharge and relapse prevention, what I needed to work on and the challenges for me. For me it's about continually challenging the voice in my head about eating and my body, the rules and the rituals I have been so used to, the guilt associated with eating and the overwhelming urge to binge or exercise. I feel like I'll need to stick to my meal plan for the next 20 years in order to survive, but if that's what I need to do, then so be it. If it releases me from this torture, then I'll do it. But this in itself will be the challenge – will I be able to keep it up? God I hope so.

Monday 29th November

I talked to Sharon about my anxieties – there seem to be so many I didn't know where to start. Was I always this anxious? I talked about school anxieties, how I hated being at school, although I never knew why. I hated the thought of school and felt sick every Sunday evening.

I still hear the theme tune of *Murder, She Wrote* and feel that nausea. I spoke about my difficulty in Scotland to make conversation. I did not have a clue what to say and usually ended up asking questions about people all the time. I wanted to be genuine and not false, with no bitchiness, and superficial chit chat irritated me. I sound like a lot of fun, don't I? No wonder I struggle. I finally spoke about my parents, about my anxiety to ask for help. I know my mum said that her mum never helped her so I'm left to believe I shouldn't ask either, and she always said that people ask too much of my dad – maybe I'm one of them? I want to be independent but I'm scared of the responsibility; I want to do it all and be in control but I'm struggling; I want people to see me as strong and dependable but I don't feel it. I feel a mess.

And before I end, I just want to say how much I detest Art Therapy sessions! I find them so difficult; I have no idea what to do, and my skills as far as art goes are very limited so it is extremely hard to produce something of any worth and compared to the girls around me who are very talented, I feel stupid and worthless.

Tuesday 30th November

Well, I've set a record at the Centre for the being the person getting onto Level 4 the quickest. Usually clients only have a couple of weeks in the flat but I'm going to be there for just over a month!

Wednesday 1st December

OK, so I know I said I didn't want to know my weight (and I don't); I just want to know what's happening. Apparently I've maintained my weight for the last three weeks. Really happy that I haven't put anything on (although I hate to say it, I fear I'll always be disappointed to know I haven't lost weight). Focus on health, focus on health!

Friday 3rd December

I've been so tempted to look at calories again. Now I'm in the flat it's so easy and, as I'm at my target weight, I really don't want to put on any more so I know I'm trying to take back some control again. I'm desperately trying to vary my snacks but I find myself drawn to 'safe' snacks and cooking similar types of lunch for myself. I'm really trying to challenge my habit of eating my meal from one side to the other, wiping the plate clean as I go and not being 'untidy'.

Treat yourself as if you were your best friend!

Monday 6th December

I went shopping, as I now have to make all my meals and snacks and I have to buy my own food.

Tuesday 7th December

In Body Image today I had to describe my relationship with my body. Um, dumpy, disproportionate, stretch-marked and saggy, insignificant, untoned, sluggish, heavier, stomach, legs, unfit, want to exercise to use pent-up energy and want to avoid my body all come to mind. Yet I would love to be comfortable with my body, to eat healthily whilst exercising for pleasure rather than as a needy obsession. Maybe one day?

I discussed my previous weekend with Sharon. I'd predicted that I would be stressed about putting up Christmas decorations, which is something I've struggled with for a while but not sure why. It was really difficult having to deal with the decorations, writing and delivering cards, sorting Christmas presents, baking, as well as helping Erin complete her school project. I just struggled to cope with loads going on and I'm scared that when I get out of here in a month I'll be responsible for the girls again and be back in the real world. I did manage to stick to my meal plan but it was really difficult as I wasn't the slightest bit hungry due to stress.

Voices in your head driving you mad?

If you can't get help to deal with them right now, choose healthy, positive distractions.

Would you want to live with an abusive, manipulating partner? Then why are you staying with Ana?

Chapter 6

RESIDENTIAL (MONTH FOUR)

Tuesday 14th December

I had huge issues with my body image when I went home at the weekend, hating the way I looked, and was desperate to do huge amounts of exercise. Whenever we're out I just don't know what to say and I feel trapped. My whole life at the moment is about food and eating and weight and exercise and blah, blah, blah, and that's all I can talk to you about because that's all I know at the moment. What I want to say is: 'But you don't want to hear about all my struggles do you? You just want to hear that I'm feeling much better now, thank you.' And when I say that, I can see the relief in your eyes.

Thursday 23rd December

There is a threat of snow so I requested to go home early for Christmas. Chris has been giving me lots of updates on the weather and he's obviously getting a bit testy as he wants to make sure I manage to get home. The girls in here are outraged because the staff called an emergency meeting for all clients, except me (I wasn't allowed to attend) and they were told that they weren't allowed to go home for Christmas – that the only way they would be able to go home would be to sign a form to say they were signing themselves out.

Tuesday 28th December

I went to a local café to meet friends and then had to leave to go back to the Centre. Rose is concerned as I have been losing weight for the last couple of weeks and she wants me to stay another week. I said no. I think it is because I am getting anxious about leaving, so losing weight is my way of controlling things. When I returned to my flat this evening the staff nurse asked me to be weighed right then – not wait until the morning, it had to be now. Not happy and it made me feel anxious. Didn't look at the scales, as I didn't want to know.

Friday 31st December

Back home for New Year's Eve. Meeting Marina, Rachel and co. at Working Men's Club for a disco. Really excited. Love a good boogie and haven't been able to 'feel' the music in a while.

Monday 3rd January

Had to go back to Aylesbury.

Wednesday 5th January

Had Care Programme Approach (CPA) meeting today, where all the staff and, it seems, everybody is discussing me and my imminent departure from the Centre.

⟡ ◆ ·◆· ◆ ⟡

What would you like to achieve in life?

What are your goals?

Write them down and then start working towards them!

⟡ ◆ ·◆· ◆ ⟡

Thursday 6th January

Went for my last session at The Oaks, where I've been volunteering each week. They gave me a card and gifts for helping them over the last few weeks. I felt overwhelmed at the kind gesture and didn't feel like I deserved it.

Went to the pub and did some karaoke for my last night. I was given cards and presents from the girls here. I'm really touched.

Friday 7th January

Home for good!

What qualities do you love
and respect in others?

Apply these rules to yourself.

You can easily love others, right?

Then why not yourself?

PART 2

WHAT HELPED ME

OK, we are now at Part 2 of this book; how did I get on after this? There is no diary but I know I continued to have struggles as well as triumphs. Eventually I achieved success, and so far, a happy ending. If you are prepared for a fight and really want to win and enjoy your own happy ending, I will share with you how. Please read on. Don't back out now – you can do this!

From my diary you can tell just how many negative thoughts I had racing around my head. Whirling around and around all day long, constantly dragging me down. My diary entries reduced during my time in Aylesbury so I am guessing that my negativity did too – although it was still there, waiting to pounce and criticise at any point.

The other observation you may have noticed was the blame I placed on others for my eating disorder. I blamed my mum, my dad, Chris, Karl, anyone who had ever been imperfect in my eyes. So much blame. I criticised myself for everything too but it was always someone else's fault. No one is perfect. I'm definitely not, although I always used to try to be. There is no instruction manual for life, unfortunately, so we just have to do our best with the resources we have at the time. That's all we can ever do.

Blame is wasted energy and only
ends up hurting you more.

You have a distorted view of yourself based on
the negative beliefs you have about yourself!

Don't trust your opinion!

Focus only on the facts.

Chapter 7

MINDFULNESS-BASED COGNITIVE THERAPY (MBCT)

When I returned home from Aylesbury I saw an eating disorders specialist every week who taught me a fantastic tool called mindfulness-based cognitive therapy (MBCT), which I still use today. I feel that it was crucial to me at this time.

MBCT is simply learning to be mindful, which helps you to become aware of any negative thoughts that enter your mind and to challenge them so that you can dismiss that thought. This thought (if it is supported by a negative belief) may return; however, if you continue to be aware and quickly challenge that thought again, it will become weaker and weaker and then you can let it go. MBCT requires determination, patience and effort. I had hundreds, if not thousands, of negative thoughts going through my mind each day. No sooner had I challenged one, another popped in. It was exhausting, and at the end of each day I'd wonder why I was so tired. But gradually, after a couple of months, I felt the negative hold on me start to slip: I was really starting to win the fight and I became more positive about life.

This is an outline of the procedure but please refer to the 'Further Resources' section to learn more.

Step One: Identify Negative Automatic Thoughts

The thoughts are based on our negative assumptions, not facts. They are often unreasonable, serve no useful purpose and can prevent you from getting better. Unfortunately, they frequently seem very believable to you and you often accept them as being the truth.

Step Two: Record Your Negative Automatic Thoughts

Write any negative thoughts down in a diary. Try to be as accurate as you can and remember what you were doing or thinking about beforehand.

Step Three: Challenging These Negative Thoughts

Take each negative thought that you have written down and ask the following questions.

- What is the evidence to support this thought? What is the evidence against it? Imagine presenting this evidence to a judge and base this on facts alone.

- What alternative, positive views could there be? How would my best friend view this situation? How would I have viewed it before I had this eating disorder? What is the evidence for these alternative views? Again, concentrate on facts!

- What if I looked at this less negatively?

- Why have I been looking at this negatively? Do I often blame myself for things when they're not my fault? Am I still punishing myself for a mistake I made before?

- Have I got high expectations of myself, expecting myself to be perfect, when others don't need to be? Am I focusing on negatives? Or comparing my life to others'?

- How can I think more positively in future?

॥ ॥ ॥ ◆ ◆ ◆ ॥ ॥ ॥

Awareness is a great thing.

With awareness we can understand what needs to change in order to improve our situation. Always try to be mindful!

॥ ॥ ॥ ◆ ◆ ◆ ॥ ॥ ॥

The transition from negative to positive will take some effort and determination but it is definitely worth it. You will start to see the gradual shift, which should encourage you to continue with this practice.

Tired? Exhausted? Freezing cold?
Hair falling out?

Constant battle going on in your head?

Choose happiness!

Your eating disorder is a way
of coping with life.

Deal with your past so you can
feel better about life.

Find another, healthier way to manage.

Chapter 8

EMOTIONAL FREEDOM TECHNIQUES (EFT)

MBCT was a great tool for me when I really needed it, and it helped a lot. It took hard work, perseverance and determination. This next tool I am going to introduce you to is quicker and needs less work, because it deals directly with your subconscious.

Unfortunately, I was introduced to EFT, or tapping as it is often called, only at the latter stage of my recovery, although it certainly helped me to continue with my recovery and address any unresolved issues. I wish I'd known about EFT from the start, before my issues became so ingrained or even during the earlier stages of recovery.

EFT resolves issues fast. This is the way to help beat the devil in your head: your eating disorder. I am so passionate about EFT and the amazing results it brings that I wish it could be taught in school – as a tool for life – so that people can use it whenever they need it.

I will loosely explain EFT to you in this section, based on my own explanations and notes from my AAMET

(Association for the Advancement of Meridian Energy Techniques) Certified Training. In Part 3, I will set out how I use it to help clients with eating disorders.

EFT can be seen as a way of rewiring the brain. When you think of a negative event, your amygdala is automatically aroused and cortisol and adrenaline are produced to assist your 'fight or flight' response. Tapping sends an electro-magnetic signal to the brain, which decreases the arousal of the amygdala and diminishes any reaction so that the association between the event and threat is broken.

EFT is explained in energy terms as releasing negative energy from the body by tapping on meridian energy points. The cause of all negative emotions is a disruption in the body's energy system. If we are terrified of public speaking and are asked to deliver a speech in front of 100 people, our body's energy system may be disrupted in that we may have a tight knot in our stomach and feel sick, and our throat may become dry. The negative emotions we feel are fear and anxiety. EFT looks to balance the disturbance in the energy system and the emotion felt so that any negative emotion is removed. The memory is still there but the association between negativity and that event is broken.

EFT was founded by Gary Craig in the 1980s; he stated that 'Every emotional state is an inside job' (Craig, 2017). This basically means that it is not what happens to you that counts but your response. Do you think you have a choice in how to respond to different situations?

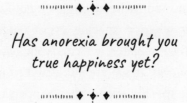

Has anorexia brought you true happiness yet?

Consider this: two people can experience the same event – let's say a car accident – at the same time, but both can have totally different responses to it. Although both may walk away unhurt, one may feel upset, tearful and have a fear of driving again. The other may just feel lucky and happy that they were not harmed at all. The reason behind the different reactions is the people themselves.

Let me explain further. We all have what Gary calls 'writings on our walls', which are attitudes, opinions and beliefs of others – from our parents, friends, colleagues, managers and whoever else may come into our lives. We learn from and listen to what these people say and we either dismiss them, or accept them as our 'truth' and they become our own beliefs.

Our first writings on our walls are from our parents, teachers and children at school and we automatically accept the things we learn from them, as we are too young to know any better. What we learn may be positive, which is great. So if someone then tries to write something negative on our wall, we can reject it as it is inconsistent with what we first learned – it doesn't sit right with us. However, if too many people overwhelm us with their negativity it may weaken our positivity and our first writings may be changed.

If we continue to be strong, self-confident, positive people, then when a specific event (such as the car accident earlier) happens, we can walk away still feeling positive. However, if we are subjected to negativity, we will interpret specific events that happen to us and use them to reinforce our negative beliefs. In the example of the car accident, we can use this to reinforce a belief that 'It always goes wrong for me' or 'I'm a bad person.' We will always look for further events to reinforce this belief and dismiss anything that contradicts it. Where things do not go wrong, we usually put this down to luck or a one-off event. This results in a negative pattern of thinking, which is difficult to 'let go'.

There are many events throughout our lives and if we have any negative beliefs about ourselves, we can easily interpret them and use them to support our negative belief. A few common negative beliefs are:

- I'm not good enough

- I'm not worthy / valuable

- I have to be perfect

- I don't fit in

- I'm always second best.

Or there could be themes around shame, guilt, approval, rejection, anger, control, etc. The list is endless.

Sometimes we may create a negative belief about ourselves based on what we thought someone said about us. When I was at school in a PE lesson, a girl in my class said to me, 'Oh Kim, I wish I had legs like yours; mine are just so skinny.' I immediately interpreted this as 'My legs are fat.' Whether she truly meant this I will never know, and I'm sure she won't even remember making the comment. The only person it affected was me, and it was only down to my lack of confidence that I wasn't able to evaluate this comment rationally and brush it aside.

To illustrate how events can help support our negative beliefs, we talk about table tops and table legs (Figure 8.1). We call our negative beliefs the table tops and we call any specific events that support this the table legs.

Figure 8.1 Table Tops and Table Legs

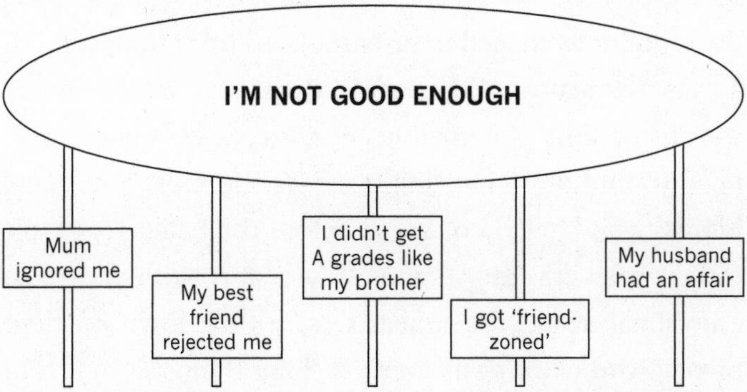

You can see that under the belief 'I'm not good enough' there are several events that support this. For example, 'My best friend rejected me', 'I got friend-zoned' and 'My husband had an affair.' However, because other events continue to support these, further variations of this negative belief can be created, for example 'I am fat and ugly', 'Nobody wants me' and 'Everyone else is better than me.'

⊹⊹⊹⊹⊹⊹⊹ ◆ ·◆· ◆ ⊹⊹⊹⊹⊹⊹⊹

You can't always be in control.

You just need to learn to surf the waves and know you'll be OK no matter what.

⊹⊹⊹⊹⊹⊹⊹ ◆ ·◆· ◆ ⊹⊹⊹⊹⊹⊹⊹

There are usually many different aspects to a specific event. In the example of domestic violence, a person could become emotional when recalling the look in someone's eyes, the smell of dinner cooking, a sinister smile or the sound of their voice. These are all different aspects and the emotion will need to be eliminated from them all.

As we saw in Figure 8.1, there are usually many specific events supporting our negative beliefs. We need to find out what events create the most emotional intensity and get rid of these before the belief (the table top) comes crashing down. If we start with the most emotional event, the others tend to fall down on their own accord without us even reaching them.

Reframing is then used, which is a new way of thinking: replacing negative beliefs with positive beliefs, leading to new writings on your walls.

If we ignore negative beliefs and let them fester, not only will we be limiting ourselves based on these beliefs but also they will surely start to grow into more negativity.

I believe that most mental and physical conditions are reactions to negative emotions that have not been dealt with. This is known as META-Health. Our brain is amazing and often tries to tell us if we need to stop and deal with something, but if we don't listen, the problem will become more persistent until it makes us stop. Often when people are asked 'When did this start? What was going on in your life around then?', they're usually able to pinpoint that it was around the time of a death in the family, a divorce or a huge responsibility that they felt overwhelmed by.

EFT can be used on the condition to help manage the symptoms, but it works best when getting to the root cause of the condition.

It is advisable that people with regular and long-term conditions continue to do EFT on themselves to avoid relapses occurring due to any negativity in the future.

You are the only one who can control your emotions and only you have the choice as to whether to deal with any negative beliefs, mental or physical conditions, etc. Other people can support you, but only you can make the choice to 'let go' and take a new path. When you are feeling emotional, it is more difficult than normal to make decisions. Yet choosing EFT can be an easier choice. Remember that if you continue on the negative path, not only will you never let go of your eating disorder, but you may also pass on your negativity to others by your 'writings on their walls'.

We tend to blame other people, but everybody has their own truth according to their own beliefs and experiences. The behaviour that a person chooses at a particular time, regardless of what it is, is the best choice available to them at that time, taking into account their personal history, beliefs, knowledge, resources and frame of reference. Again, it is our reaction that counts and we do have a choice.

So let me show you how to sample EFT.

First, try to think of a memory / event that still bothers you right now. Please do *not* think of a particularly painful issue, as I don't want to subject you to any real upset or abreaction;[1] always contact a practitioner to help with this. It may be an argument that you had with someone yesterday, an incident such as someone pulling out in front of you whilst you were driving, or perhaps an anxiety about a forthcoming event.

Either way, think of this issue and try to note what you are feeling – what your emotion is. Is it anger, fear, anxiety, disappointment, hurt, sadness, guilt or shame? (See Box 8.1 for further emotions.)

Once you have pinpointed the emotion, assess where in your body you are feeling this. Is it in your head, throat, chest, shoulder or stomach or do you feel it throughout your body? How does it feel?

Now give the emotion an intensity level from 0 to 10, with 0 being no emotion at all and 10 being the highest level of emotion you could ever possibly feel. It is important to assess the intensity level, as it gives you a starting point, and when we reassess after tapping, we can easily identify if the tapping is working.

You are ready to start tapping once:

- you have your issue

- you know what emotion you are feeling

- you know where and what it feels like

- you have given it an intensity level.

---

1   An abreaction is a person's emotional response to recalling an uncomfortable memory, which can range from feeling discomfort to having a panic attack.

When tapping, you:

- can tap using any hand

- can tap on your left side, your right side, on both or a mixture of both

- need to tap firmly

- need to tap repeatedly – around 4 times per second.

Further Negative Emotions that Might Need Working On

- Anger
- Annoyance
- Anxiety
- Boredom
- Despair
- Disappointment
- Disgust
- Doubt
- Embarrassment
- Envy
- Frustration
- Guilt

- Helplessness
- Hurt
- Irritation
- Fear
- Powerlessness
- Sadness
- Shame
- Stress
- Shock
- Tension
- Worry

⬥ ⬥ ⬥

Whenever you feel the pull to go back, remember these behaviours never made you happy.

⬥ ⬥ ⬥

The Tapping Sequence

We start with what we call the 'Set Up' statement, which attempts to eliminate any reason you may have for holding on to this issue. For example, releasing any anger towards someone may actually unmask feelings of our own hurt, fear, shame or guilt that we'd rather not feel and, hence, we subconsciously want to hold on to the anger.

We tap on the karate chop point, the underside soft part of the hand where we would do a 'karate chop' (see Figure 8.2) and say the Set Up statement: 'Even though I have [this emotion], I completely love and accept myself.' You need to say this three times. I know this might sound silly, but it is basically saying that you acknowledge and accept your feelings and you also accept yourself for having these feelings. Some people feel very awkward saying 'I love and accept myself', so if you prefer you can say something like 'I'm OK' or 'I'd like to love and accept myself.' Remember, however, EFT works on the basis that you're trying to shift energy, and the more resolve you have, the more success you'll have. Just try saying 'I love and accept myself', even if you feel uncomfortable; this won't always be the case. You need to substitute '[this emotion]' in the set up statement for whatever emotion it is that you're feeling, for example anger, hurt or fear.

Once you have completed the Set Up three times, start tapping on each of the tapping points, one at a time (see Figure 8.3 for a diagram of tapping points), tapping firmly and briskly on each point for a few seconds before moving to the next. Start at the top of the head and finish at the karate chop point, tapping on every point. Whilst tapping, you need to focus on the emotion or issue that you're working on; so, for example, if it was a Level 5 anger in your stomach, you'd say (as you tapped on each point) one of the following: 'this anger', 'this Level 5 anger', 'this anger in my stomach', 'this Level 5 anger in my stomach' or 'this Level 5 anger raging in my stomach'. Substitute these words for the specifics of what you are feeling right now.

Here is the tapping points sequence with the abbreviations that are used for each point:

- TH: Top of head (place your hand on the crown of your head)

- EB: Inside of your eyebrow (where your eyebrow starts)

- SE: Side of your eye (on the bony part)

- UE: Under your eye (on the bony part)

- UN: Under your nose (on the dip between your nose and top of your mouth)

- CH: On your chin, under your mouth (on the dip between your mouth and top of your chin)

- CB: Collar bone (about four fingers left or right from where a tie would be knotted)

- UA: Under arm (in line with the nipple, 4 inches under the armpit)

- Thumb: Side of thumb (on the part where the nail and skin meet)

- F1: Side of 1st finger (on the part where the nail and skin meet)

- F2: Side of 2nd finger (on the part where the nail and skin meet)

- F3: Side of 3rd finger (on the part where the nail and skin meet)

- F4: Side of 4th finger (on the part where the nail and skin meet)

- KC: Karate chop point (underside, soft part of hand).

Seeking help can be scary, but the alternative could be much worse.

Figure 8.2 Karate chop point

Illustration by Hayley Reynolds (www.artisthayleyreynolds.co.uk)

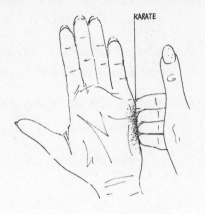

Figure 8.3 Tapping Points

Illustration by Hayley Reynolds (www.artisthayleyreynolds.co.uk)

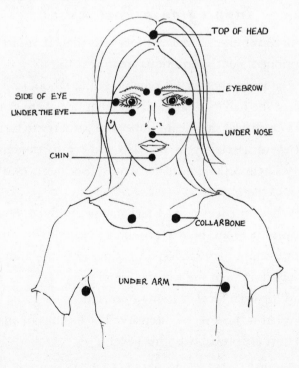

꙰꙰꙰꙰꙰ ◆ ·◆· ◆ ꙰꙰꙰꙰꙰

*Our mind is more powerful than
a thousand computers.*

*Our eating disorder is like the
most deadly of viruses.*

*But the computer can be reprogrammed
and repaired, and so can we!*

꙰꙰꙰꙰꙰ ◆ ·◆· ◆ ꙰꙰꙰꙰꙰

Here are two specific examples to allow you to understand completely.

Tapping on a Past Event

My first example is a real memory (one that I have already mentioned) but the emotions are now fictitious.

The issue/memory is when a girl at school said she wished she had legs like mine and that hers were skinny, and I presumed she meant mine were fat. I try to picture this event as clearly as possible and try to remember every single detail. I hear her words. I see her eyes when she says them.

What do I feel now? I feel shame and hurt. Shame because there are people around to hear this comment and I assume they are looking at my legs too, and hurt because I thought she was my friend.

Where can I feel it? In my stomach.

What is the level of intensity? The feelings of shame and hurt are probably both a Level 6.

I now tap on my karate chop point and say my Set Up statement three times: *'Even though I feel this shame and hurt in my stomach and it's a Level 6 when I think back to my memory from school, I completely love and accept myself.'*

I then tap the sequence:

TH: *'This shame'*

EB: *'This hurt'*

SE: *'Level 6 hurt and shame'*

UE: *'I feel it all in my stomach'*

UN: *'Shame and hurt from this memory from school'*

CH: *'Level 6 hurt and shame'*

CB: *'This shame'*

UA: *'This hurt'*

Thumb: *'I feel it all in my stomach'*

F1: *'She said she wanted legs like mine'*

F2: *'She said hers were skinny'*

F3: *'I thought she meant my legs were fat'*

F4: *'And I still feel shame and hurt'*

KC: *'Level 6 hurt and shame'*

After tapping a sequence, I take a deep breath. I again try to picture the event as clearly as possible, hearing her words and seeing her eyes. How do I feel now? I can remember the event but it seems more distant, slightly blurry and the emotion doesn't feel as sharp. I still have some hurt but I don't feel shame now; in fact, I feel a little angry at myself because I may have misinterpreted her words and I've carried this for so long. Again, I feel the emotions in my stomach. The hurt is a Level 3 and the anger at myself is Level 4.

Once again, I tap on the karate chop point and say the Set Up statement three times: *'Even though I have this remaining hurt and anger at Level 3 and 4 and I feel it in my stomach when I think about my memory from school, I completely love and accept myself.'*

I tap the sequence again:

TH: *'This remaining hurt'*

EB: *'This remaining anger'*

SE: *'This remaining Level 3 and 4 hurt and anger'*

UE: *'I feel it all in my stomach'*

UN: *'This remaining hurt and anger from this memory from school'*

CH: *'This remaining Level 3 and 4 hurt and anger'*

CB: *'She said she wanted legs like mine'*

UA: *'She said hers were skinny'*

Thumb: *'I don't know what she meant because I assumed and never checked what she meant'*

F1: *'I lived all my life with this negative comment and it was probably a compliment'*

F2: 'I know my legs were fine'

F3: 'I wasted emotions over this comment'

F4: 'But I let them go now'

KC: 'I let go of the hurt and anger'

I take another deep breath and check how I feel once again. If I still feel any hurt or anger, or if another emotion comes up, I repeat the above sequence.

I continue to tap and state any thoughts that come into my mind, as if I am telling a friend the story of what happened and how I feel now.

Choose life!

Tapping on Physical Pain

The second example shows how to use EFT on physical pain. Oh yes, it can be done. Although the example shown below is totally fictitious, it is very representative of what can happen in EFT when you're working on physical pain.

I start again by assessing how I am feeling. I have pain in my shoulder. As it is pain, I need to try to be as specific as possible so I ask myself:

• Where exactly is the pain?

- What type of pain is it?

- What does it feel like?

- If the pain were a colour or shape, what would it be?

- If the pain were an emotion, what would it be?

- If the pain were a person, who would it be?

- What level of pain is it on a scale of 0 to 10?

After moving around and trying to assess the pain, I describe the pain as being like someone dragging a sharp pencil against my skin about 6 cm down from the top of my shoulder in the middle of my right side. I cannot describe the pain in terms of colour or shape but if the pain were an emotion I would guess it would be anger. I'm not sure who the pain would be. The level of pain is a 7.

I now tap on my karate chop point and say my Set Up statement three times: *'Even though I feel this dragging pain in the top middle of my right shoulder and it's a Level 7 and I think it might be anger, I completely love and accept myself.'*

I then tap the sequence:

TH: 'This dragging pain in my shoulder'

EB: 'This pain in the top middle of my right shoulder'

SE: 'Level 7 pain'

UE: 'This pain that may be anger'

UN: 'This dragging pain downwards about 6cm from the top middle of my right shoulder'

CH: *'Like someone dragging a sharp pencil down my shoulder'*

CB: *'And I'm angry'*

UA: *'This Level 7 pain'*

Thumb: *'This dragging pain'*

F1: *'Dragging me down'*

F2: *'Who's dragging me down?'*

F3: *'Who am I angry at for dragging me down?'*

F4: *'This Level 7 pain'*

KC: *'This dragging pain in my left shoulder'*

After tapping a sequence, I take a deep breath. Once again, I try to assess the pain. I can still feel some pain but it has moved: it is now in the right side of my neck and it is a Level 4. There is still a slight dragging feeling but less than before.

So I tap again on the karate chop point and say the Set Up statement three times: *'Even though I feel this remaining dragging pain in the right side of my neck and it's a Level 4 and I still think it might be anger, I completely love and accept myself.'*

I then tap the sequence:

TH: *'This remaining dragging pain in my neck'*

EB: *'This remaining pain in the right side of my neck'*

SE: *'This remaining Level 4 pain'*

UE: 'This remaining pain that may be anger'

UN: 'This remaining slight dragging pain downwards in the right side of my neck'

CH: 'Like someone dragging a pencil down my shoulder'

CB: 'And I'm still angry'

UA: 'This remaining Level 4 pain'

Thumb: 'This remaining dragging pain'

F1: 'Still dragging me down a bit'

F2: 'Who's dragging me down?'

F3: 'Who am I angry at for dragging me down?'

F4: 'Who is a pain in my neck?'

KC: 'This remaining dragging pain in the right side of my neck'

I take another deep breath and check how I feel. I then realise that this pain started when a colleague at work started doing less work and I had to do more than my fair share. I felt that he was dragging me down and I was under pressure to do his work as well as my own. I felt as if I was sinking and could not cope. I was angry that he was quite happy to sit back and let me! Now I know what is causing the pain, I ignore any remaining physical pain and tap on any anger I feel about this colleague, using the above sequence.

When the emotion of anger has cleared, I will be able to see more clearly and realise that I do have a choice, which is to talk to my colleague, or my manager if necessary, in order to rectify the situation. After dealing with the emotions surrounding this issue, the physical pain will be reduced even more and may even be eliminated.

〰️ ◆ ·◆· ◆ 〰️

All the negative thoughts you are holding on to are keeping you trapped like a prisoner.

How would it feel to step out of your 'prison cell'?

Exciting? Scary? Unsafe?

What if you could step out whilst feeling in control and confident?

Would you want to?

〰️ ◆ ·◆· ◆ 〰️

Now I have explained it to you and given you a couple of examples, have a go yourself.

Remember, you need to:

- think of a memory / event that still bothers you or focus on a physical pain you are feeling

- work out what exactly you are feeling and where

- work out what level of intensity this feeling/pain is at

- start tapping on the karate chop point saying the Set Up statement three times

- tap the tapping sequence.

When people do EFT on themselves, they become concerned about the correct words to use. Do not worry about the words. As long as you feel the feeling inside your body, you can tap and say nothing – it will still work. Alternatively, if you wish to rant about the day you have had or go through any anxieties about something that is happening that day, just go ahead. Talking and tapping is great because you are still tuning into your body and feeling the emotions.

See how you get on with a few minor issues and remember to write down the level of intensity at the start, as sometimes, particularly if you are new to this, you may not believe that your anger went from an 8 to a 4 in just a couple of rounds of tapping.

Imagine bundling up all your negative
thoughts about yourself and others.

Even if you feel justified in holding on to
them, they are only hurting you, no one else.

You need to let them go. You have
the power to let them go.

Imagine throwing these thoughts off the
top of a cliff or setting them on fire.

You are worthy. You are amazing.

You are special. You are unique.

You deserve to be happy as
much as anyone else.

Happiness doesn't come from
anyone else but you.

Believe in yourself!

Eating is necessary for survival.

It is not a luxury item.

There is nothing to feel guilty about!

PART 3

HELPING YOU KISS GOODBYE TO ANA

Chapter 9

HOW OTHERS CAN HELP

First Things First

You may be reading this after having been in residential treatment several times, or not having even visited your GP yet. No matter where you are in terms of recovery, you need to admit to yourself there is an issue that requires outside help.

Due to the denial and secrecy around an eating disorder, often we are not aware ourselves that there is a problem until we become pretty rigid in our thinking around food and weight. We have already developed rules and rituals in our behaviours that we fear losing because they seem to make us feel safe and in control.

The thing that is most important right now is to ask yourself: 'Do I want to feel better?' It is absolutely normal to feel scared, to feel conflicted and to even question whether you will ever feel better. Do you want to try?

If you do, great. That's a brilliant start! What you need to realise is that there are people who can help you, support you and teach you techniques in order to help. However, no one can fix you and no one can make you feel better if you don't want to. It is reflected in the phrase 'You can lead a horse to water but you can't make it drink.'

I remember being offered counselling and, although I was convinced at the time that it did not work, for me, this was an excuse. I just was not ready.

So is recovery possible? Yes, of course, but it's not easy, and it requires working on the root cause rather than solely on eating disorder behaviours.

I have worked with many clients who have each transformed their lives by taking responsibility for their own recovery. They treated their recovery like a project and worked hard to achieve great results.

You do have options if you are willing to try to I will share some suggested support ideas later in the book. Some are available through the NHS and are free but some require investment in terms of money. All will require investment in terms of time and effort.

I find that the NHS is extremely under-resourced and waiting-list times are very long, so if you find yourself in this situation, please do consider looking for alternative paid therapies. Yes, you may have to pay but it can definitely be worth it. I waited a long time before I sought other help and my options reduced as a result. I was told by a counsellor who specialised in eating disorders that I was too ill for her to be able to help me. At this point, I felt totally alone and that there was no way out. Don't let this happen to you. Try to reach out for help now, as it is often the case that the quicker you get help, the better the chance of recovery.

〟〟〟〟〟 ◆ ◆ ◆ 〟〟〟〟〟

*How many people do you
compare yourself with?*

*Do you really know that they're
happy and content?*

*For all you know, they could be comparing
themselves with you and feeling inadequate!*

〟〟〟〟〟 ◆ ◆ ◆ 〟〟〟〟〟

Parents and Family

You may be feeling like you are trapped in a torturous place, but your family and friends are also in a desperate situation. They want to wave a magic wand and make it all go away but they cannot. And the person they are trying to help, the person they love – you – will not accept this help and you are pushing them away. I totally understand this, I was the same. However, imagine how you would feel in their situation if you were trying to help someone who did not want your help.

Parents and carers can also learn EFT to address their own anxieties, frustration, anger, feelings of guilt and powerlessness. This will help them feel calmer and more in control in order to help you more effectively. Their efforts will be more positive, rather than just reactions, and this will help stop the situation turning into an argument or a battle of wills.

If you want to feel better, you need to accept that things will have to change, which is scary. But unless you can communicate to your family and friends about how you are feeling, they will never be able to even try to understand. Tell them what your fears are, what might help to alleviate these and what definitely will not. Tell them that although you may express an idea you feel might help initially, if you are feeling anxious this may not be of help at a later stage. That is why EFT is so important: you can all 'tap' to eliminate anxieties, allowing everyone to feel calmer and less pressured in order to keep making progress.

For me, my biggest fears were trying to change the food that I ate each day. Whether it was something different or eating a slightly larger portion, the result would be the same. I would feel so guilty that I usually ended up bingeing. Knowing someone was there – distracting me from a potential binge and doing EFT with me to eliminate the guilt and feelings of failure – would help enormously.

It was also important for me to feel safe, to trust people and to know that all they wanted was for me to be healthy, not for me to be fat. I needed to know that they were encouraging me to eat healthy foods.

Why don't you get your family and friends to try EFT for themselves by following the example that you did in Chapter 8? If they are sceptical, tell them that you feel this could really help you and them.

Once they witness the benefits, they may like to work through their own issues and fears with an EFT practitioner too.

Talking Treatments

The information in the following sections is paraphrased from the NHS website and the mental health charity Mind's website. For more information, see the 'Further Resources' section.

There are many different types of talking treatments available but they all focus on helping you to cope with your emotions and the things that happen in your life.

They involve talking to a therapist about your thoughts and feelings and helping you understand these feelings and behaviour better. This can help you to change your behaviour or the way you feel about things, if you'd like.

Talking treatments can help with:

- mental health problems

- physical health problems

- difficult emotions

- difficult experiences.

Cognitive Analytical Therapy (CAT)

CAT involves looking at how you currently cope with emotional stress and difficulties in your life, to find unhelpful patterns of behaviour and to create new coping strategies.

CAT is an active therapy and you will normally be expected to keep a diary and do some homework between sessions. You will need to provide background information.

The therapist will:

- help you to recognise patterns of behaviour and to understand where these have come from

- write a letter to try to sum up the main patterns and the targets of therapy

- use diagrams to describe the main patterns of behaviour, thinking and feelings that you wish to change.

(Mind, 2016)

What are you hoping that the scales will tell you today?

Is it ever going to be enough to make you feel better about yourself?

Interpersonal Therapy (IPT)

IPT is a time-limited and structured psychotherapy for moderate to severe depression. Psychological symptoms, such as depressed mood, can be understood as a response to current difficulties in our everyday interactions with others. In turn, the depressed mood can also affect the quality of our relationships.

IPT focuses on difficulties in relating to others and helping the person to identify how they are feeling and behaving in their relationships. When a person is able to interact more effectively, their psychological symptoms often improve. (See Mind, 2016; NHS Choices, 2016a.)

Cognitive Behavioural Therapy (CBT)

CBT focuses on how your thoughts, beliefs and attitudes affect your feelings and behaviour. Any negative thinking patterns and behaviour can be changed using a combination of cognitive therapy (examining the things you think) and behaviour therapy (examining the things you do).

CBT is based on the idea that the way we think about situations can affect the way we feel and behave. If you interpret situations negatively, and your negative interpretation goes unchallenged, these patterns in your thoughts, feelings and behaviour can become part of a continuous cycle. (See Mind, 2016; NHS Choices, 2016b.)

Dialectical Behaviour Therapy (DBT)

DBT is based on CBT but has been adapted for those who experience emotions very intensely.

DBT helps you to change unhelpful behaviours, but it differs from CBT in that it also focuses on accepting who you are at the same time. It helps you learn to manage your difficult emotions by letting yourself experience, recognise and accept them. Then, as you learn to accept and regulate your emotions, you also become more able to change your harmful behaviour. To help you achieve this, DBT therapists use a balance of acceptance and change techniques. (See Mind, 2016; NHS Choices, 2016c.)

Take one meal at a time.

Take one bite at a time.

Stay strong. Keep breathing. You can do this!

Do you struggle to socialise? Don't panic!

Why have you got to impress these people?

Just be yourself.

That's totally good enough.

When you have a setback, don't give up.

You haven't gone back to the beginning;
you've just stepped back a little.

You've come so far, you're still progressing.

Don't stop!

Chapter 10

HOW I CAN HELP

As I have already mentioned, when I was really struggling with anorexia, I felt as if I was at the bottom of the deepest, darkest well with not even a chink of light shining through. I was desperate for help and caught in a cycle of bingeing and restricting, and it became safer not to try. I was at a stage where every half hour I had to think of reasons not to 'take the easy way out'. I had two daughters and knew things needed to change, but I did not know how and I had more or less given up trying.

When I reached out in the past I was made to feel that I was not ill enough or that help was just not available. I became worse and was eventually offered residential treatment. Although I was scared, I looked forward to being able to try to eat, knowing that I could not binge afterwards. All the time I was there I kept repeating to myself: 'I need to trust that they won't make me fat.'

I wasted years of my life not getting help because I was scared: scared of losing control and scared of people noticing my behaviours and trying to suggest things that I could not do. I just wanted to feel safe. In reality, I was not safe at all. I was in danger of losing my life, but I am not sure I even cared. I just wanted to feel safe.

Hence, I know how it feels. I know how hard it is to live with an eating disorder, although I know that the thought of recovery is difficult too: it sounded unimaginable and I was convinced that the furthest I would ever get was following strict meal plans for the rest of my life, just managing my anorexia. But I got further than I ever dreamt, and so can you! I would love to share my personal experience and knowledge with you and offer you the best way I know of how to get to that place where you feel relaxed around eating, food and your weight with no feelings of guilt or fear. I want to share with you how you can get to a place where you still feel safe and in control and do not focus on BMI or meal plans.

This will help you to:

- enjoy a full and active life with family, friends and work

- not think constantly about food and trying to lose more weight

- be free of the voice in your head

- feel that you are good enough, you are worthy and you have a sense of purpose

- feel that you belong

- feel happy and content with yourself.

Because I work with mindsets, I look to remove the negative beliefs you have about yourself and any past events that you are still struggling with so that you can feel more confident and more positive about yourself. Whilst doing this, the need to use anorexic behaviours in order to stay safe and in control will become weaker and easier to let go of.

⅏⅏⅏ ♦ ·♦· ♦ ⅏⅏⅏

Ana feeds on manipulating, controlling and ultimately destroying you.

Whilst you starve yourself, Ana lives.

Choose life. Choose you!

⅏⅏⅏ ♦ ·♦· ♦ ⅏⅏⅏

Eating disorders are not about food, eating or weight. These are the symptoms. They are about trying to cope with or control our emotions, usually as a result of past experiences. When we get to the root cause, permanent recovery becomes possible.

Now, let us make a start, and the best place to start is with any denial that you may still feel. I had huge denial, convincing myself that there was not an issue and that I was just not hungry. The first exercise is to answer some questions honestly. Consider the question: 'Do I really have anorexia?'

Do I Really Have Anorexia?

There is often a lot of denial around anorexia. We think we are in control and do not want to lose that by seeking help and being told what to do by someone else. We can tell ourselves that we are fine and any doubts that something may be wrong are quickly banished by the anorexic voice in our head telling us that our current behaviours are fine, to just stay strong, keep focused and all will be good.

So, how do we know if there is a problem? Let us have a look at the following questions and answer them honestly.

Accepting there is an issue can be scary, but this is the first step towards feeling free, happy, confident and positive. You can do this!

- Do negative thoughts about food, eating, weight, exercise or your body image affect your life every day?

- How often do you think about food/eating/weight/body image?

- Do you have rules and rituals regarding food, eating, exercising, weighing yourself, body checking or anything else?

- Do you dislike/hate your body?

- How often do you compare yourself to others?

- Are you uncomfortable at (or do you avoid) mealtimes or socialising?

- Do you feel scared/worried/guilty about eating/ food?

- Do you feel scared/worried/guilty after eating/ food?

- Do voices in your head make you feel guilty or anxious about eating?

- Do you feel tortured by food?

- Do you eat in secret?

- Do you restrict even when you are hungry in order to control your weight?

- Do you sometimes eat big quantities of food un- controllably?

- Have you purged after this?

- Have you forgotten what 'normal' eating is?

- Do you regularly 'need' to exercise even when you are exhausted?

- Do you use extreme methods to lose weight?

- How often do you weigh yourself?

Did you answer 'yes', 'frequently' or 'at least every day' to most of them? If so, I would suggest that there could be an issue that you may need help with. I am guessing you already realise this, but it is important to accept if you want to move forward.

Negative or Limiting Beliefs

I would like to provide you with some insight into the root cause and why it is so hard for you to let go of your anorexia. This involves going over the negative or limiting beliefs you have about yourself.

Up to the age of six or seven years old, we are in a very observational state and notice everything that goes on around us. It doesn't need to be spoken, as we are very good at reading body language. Because of our age, our main observations are of our parents, siblings, teachers and children from school. Now, if we grow up in a positive environment, we tend to grow up to be confident, positive people. But if Mum or Dad has negative beliefs or fears of their own, or is struggling with their own mental health issue, we can take on their beliefs as our own. We interpret all events that happen and form beliefs based on their beliefs. So if a girl from school makes fun of how we look in front of the whole class, we might interpret this to mean 'I am ugly' or 'Attention is bad.'

Once we have these beliefs ingrained, we will go through life looking for further events to support these beliefs. We will absolutely disregard any events happening that suggest we are not ugly or that receiving attention is good. We will dismiss them as not being important, not being real or being a one-off. And we will focus solely on the negatives. We need to remove these negative beliefs in order to stop focusing on the negatives in our lives.

See the table below for a list of typical negative beliefs. As you read them to yourself, I want you to use your gut reaction to see if you respond to any of them, because if you do, it is likely that you have this belief about yourself.

Make a note against each one that resonates with you, and give it a grading of 0 to 10, where 0 feels not at all true and 10 feels completely true. Do not spend too much time overthinking this, just put down a figure that comes to mind. Also, do not feel overwhelmed if you tick the majority of the beliefs, because once we start working on one belief, it will have a knock-on effect on the others and they will reduce as well.

Common Negative Beliefs
(Intensity level: 0 = Not at all true; 10 = Completely true)

	Limiting belief	Intensity level 0–10	Any qualifying comments
1	I am ashamed		
2	I am worthless		
3	I don't deserve to be loved		
4	I don't deserve to be happy		
5	I don't deserve to be successful		
6	I don't deserve to be healthy		
7	I always get it wrong		
8	No one likes me		
9	I am not good enough		
10	Everyone else is better than me		
11	I don't like myself		
12	I have done something really terrible		
13	I am angry		

14	It isn't right to show anger		
15	It's not fair		
16	Everyone else gets more than me		
17	It is all their fault		
18	They always let me down		
19	I always let myself down		
20	I have to be perfect		
21	I have to do it all myself		
22	I am afraid		
23	I am anxious		
24	I need to be in control		
25	Something terrible is going to happen		
26	There is no point in trying		
27	I am not safe in the world		
28	I can't trust anyone		
29	I can't trust myself		
30	I have to keep them happy		
31	Bad things always happen if I am happy		
32	I cannot ever be healthy		
33	It is not safe to show my emotions		

Source: Phoenix EFT, www.phoenixeft.co.uk

How did you find that? Well done – you have just taken a great step towards identifying your root causes. Now, take a look at what you have written. These beliefs are ruling and limiting your life. Can you see how you are always focusing on things that happen where you feel 'Everyone else is better than me', 'I have to be perfect', 'I need to be in control' or 'I have to do it all myself'? Can you see how these beliefs are creating rules for you to live by and are keeping you trapped in your negativity? You need to get rid of these beliefs in order to be free of these rules and your anorexia, and I can help you do this.

‖‖‖‖‖‖‖ ◆ ⋅◆⋅ ◆ ‖‖‖‖‖‖‖

Recovery is about feeling confident and positive about yourself.

It won't be linked to your weight or how you think you look in the mirror.

‖‖‖‖‖‖‖ ◆ ⋅◆⋅ ◆ ‖‖‖‖‖‖‖

The following worksheet can be downloaded so you can fill it out: www.jkp.com/catalogue/book/9781785924644.

Questionnaire

I have provided some questions to get you thinking about key events in your life that may have contributed towards your anorexia.

Besides thinking about where those negative beliefs came from, we also need to look at questions such as the following.

1. When did you first struggle with eating, food, your body and your weight? What was happening in your life around then?

2. Does anyone else in your family have an eating disorder or issues with eating, food, body image or weight?

3. What are the positives of anorexia? How does it keep you safe?

4. What are the negatives of not having anorexia?

5. If there was an event in your life that you wish didn't happen, what would it be?

6. What would happen if you were entirely without this eating disorder?

7. What emotions do you feel that you are trying to control with your eating disorder? What are you hoping that controlling your weight will help you with?

8. What past events are you still battling with?

9. What do the voices in your head say to you about you, your weight, eating, food, exercise, your body and anything else?

10. When are you most likely to severely restrict or binge? What are the triggers?

11. What have you struggled with or are you struggling to control in your life?

12. What would you focus on if you weren't thinking about food, weight, exercise, etc.?

13. How do you feel about yourself?

14. What emotions do you regularly feel, for example fear, guilt, shame, anger or hate?

As an example, my responses would have been as follows.

1. When did you first struggle with eating, food, your body and your weight? What was happening in your life around then?

    a. I first struggled with eating when I was forced to eat meals. I remember sitting on my own at the table, feeling guilty, bad and angry.

    b. I first had an issue with my body when a girl from school said she wished she had legs like mine and that hers were too skinny. I thought she was saying that mine were fat.

    c. I first had a real issue with my weight when I put on weight during pregnancy. I felt hunger like I had never felt before and ballooned in size. I found it difficult to lose weight after giving birth and my weight caused me to have a huge lack of confidence and low self-esteem.

2. Does anyone else in your family have an eating disorder or issues with eating, food, body image or weight?

My dad definitely uses food in order to stuff down his emotions but I wouldn't say he has an eating disorder.

3. What are the positives of anorexia? How does it keep you safe?

I felt in control when I was able to restrict. I was able to hide away. I felt special. I felt powerful.

4. What are the negatives of not having anorexia?

I felt scared that I would lose control and become fat. I was scared people would think I was recovered when I was not. I was worried people would comment on my weight and say how healthy I looked, which I interpret as meaning I looked fat. I would not be special anymore because I would lose my anorexic identity.

5. If there was an event in your life that you wish didn't happen, what would it be?

My ex-husband having an affair and leaving straight away. There was no remorse and no explanation – not a word.

6. What would happen if you were entirely without this eating disorder?

> Again, I felt scared of losing control, which was my way of coping. I struggled to see that I could reach any positives. I just didn't believe it.

⦁⦁⦁⦁⦁⦁ ◆ ·◆· ◆ ⦁⦁⦁⦁⦁⦁

When you're desperate to restrict,
just keep telling yourself:

I know I can choose to restrict
and lose weight – but did I really
feel happy at my lowest weight?

Choose happiness!

⦁⦁⦁⦁⦁⦁ ◆ ·◆· ◆ ⦁⦁⦁⦁⦁⦁

7. What emotions do you feel that you are trying to control with your eating disorder? What are you hoping that controlling your weight will help you with?

> I was trying to avoid emotions caused by my ex-husband's affair. I could not control this situation so I controlled my weight.

8. What past events are you still battling with?

> a. I struggled with issues around my mum's mental health.

> b. I struggled with my dad's perceived lack of expressed affection.

    c. I struggled with my failure to move away from the town I grew up in.

9. What do the voices in your head say to you about you, your weight, eating, food, exercise, your body and anything else?

> That I was not special; I did not belong; I had no purpose; I was second best; I was fat and ugly; I had to restrict, otherwise I would fail; I could only eat safe foods; I needed to exercise even if I felt exhausted.

10. When are you most likely to severely restrict or binge? What are the triggers?

> Restriction was easiest when I was busy; hence I did not want to stop. Bingeing came after trying to eat something new or in addition to my normal safe intake, or if I restricted for a long period of time and I was tortured by the thoughts of food. I would even dream that I had eaten something really bad and I would wake up in a panic. The relief of knowing it was just a dream was unbelievable.

11. What have you struggled with or are you struggling to control in your life?

> This was my ex-husband's affair and the responsibility of being a single mum of two.

12. What would you focus on if you weren't thinking about food, weight, exercise, etc.?

At the time it was about how rejected and hurt I felt about being abandoned by my ex-husband and the anger about being left to raise our two girls. I felt that we had made the decision to have children together and he had just decided he did not want to do it anymore and buggered off.

13. How do you feel about yourself?

I felt like I was nothing special – not important – and people were better off without me; I was a burden; I was inferior to others.

14. What emotions do you regularly feel, for example fear, guilt, shame, anger or hate?

I felt fear about raising the girls and coping on my own; I felt hurt and sad that my girls did not have their dad around; I felt confused by how he had treated me. I felt anxious about food and socialising so I withdrew from people around me; I felt helpless and powerless about my situation.

You will see that answering these questions has shown how there were things that happened in my life that contributed to my beliefs and to my anorexia.

Go through this list of questions yourself and make a note of anything you feel might be relevant. But please, I don't want you to upset yourself by thinking about or digging up any traumatic memories. I don't want you to go there. You know about these anyway and the fact that you are aware of what needs to be addressed in order to move forward is enough. I just want you to think about other non-traumatic events that have happened that may have contributed to your eating disorder.

⚬⚬⚬⚬⚬⚬ ◆ ◆ ◆ ⚬⚬⚬⚬⚬⚬

Why do you demand so much of yourself?

Do you place such high expectations on others?

⚬⚬⚬⚬⚬⚬ ◆ ◆ ◆ ⚬⚬⚬⚬⚬⚬

Introducing EFT Again

I will now introduce you to EFT, or tapping, again. Of course, I have explained it before in more generic terms but it is really important for me to explain it in detail. This is the tool that changed my life, and it can change yours too.

Now, I need to be honest and stress that tapping is really powerful; however, you still need to use it a few times a day in order to really make a difference. Do not expect to tap for a minute and then to be absolutely fine. You will still need to put in the effort, and when you do, it will be very effective.

Can you remember how tapping works? If you were not that keen on public speaking and I asked you to give a speech in front of 100 people, chances are you would start to feel sick, your heart would start racing and you may have a dry throat and sweaty palms. The emotion you would feel is fear or anxiety. We call it negative energy in our body and we tap on meridian energy points in order to let this negative energy and these emotions go, in order to feel more calm and relaxed.

We can use tapping to eliminate negative emotions from past, future and current events.

I'm going to guide you through a typical tapping session and I want you to tap the points and read the words out loud. If you notice any protests, objections or niggles, make a note of these, as they are blocks that need to be addressed. For example, this tapping script includes the following statement: 'If I could let go of the negatives, I could be more positive.' When reading this statement, the voice in your head may protest with 'I don't believe it's possible', 'It sounds too difficult', 'Yes but I've tried before and it didn't work' or 'What if I can't?' Write these thoughts down, as they can also be tapped on. If any words I have used in the scripts do not resonate with you, please use your own.

The tapping sequence is as follows:

Set Up

Karate chop point: 'Even though I have [this emotion], I completely love and accept myself.' Say this three times.

The Sequence

Tapping points:

- TH: Top of head

- EB: Inside of your eyebrow

- SE: Side of your eye

- UE: Under your eye

- UN: Under your nose

- CH: On your chin, under your mouth

- CB: Collar bone

- UA: Under arm

- Thumb: Side of thumb

- F1: Side of 1st finger

- F2: Side of 2nd finger

- F3: Side of 3rd finger

- F4: Side of 4th finger

- KC: Karate chop point.

See Figures 8.2 and 8.3 if you need a reminder of where these points are.

The 'What to Work On' worksheet later in this chapter will help you identify the issue you would like to work on. I have provided suggestions of challenging eating disorder behaviours that you can choose if you so wish. However, as I have previously stated, that is not how I start working. That is not my priority.

I have chosen 'How I'm feeling today' to give you an example. Think about how you feel right now. What emotions are you feeling? There could be a mixture of emotions and it is always best to take one issue at a time. For the sake of this example, I will include a few possibilities. Where do you feel this emotion in your body? What does it feel like? What is the level of intensity (0–10, where 0 = nothing and 10 = it could not go any higher)?

To start, tap on the points and say the words out loud. As directed, tap on the karate chop point for the first three statements (the set up) before proceeding with the rest of the tapping sequence, until you've finished the tapping script. Then take a few deep breaths and assess how you're now feeling. Start tapping again as before, but include any new emotions and feelings that you're experiencing, and continue ideally until the level of intensity is 0 but at least until the level is 3.

KC: 'Even though I feel tortured in my stomach because I can't stop thinking about food, I completely love and accept myself'

KC: 'Even though I feel so tortured by food at the moment, I completely love and accept myself'

KC: 'Even though I feel tortured in my stomach because I'm struggling to focus on anything but food, I completely love and accept myself'

TH: 'I feel like I'm in the deepest, darkest well'

EB: 'Every time I try to climb out, I fall back down and hurt myself'

SE: 'It always ends up worse'

UE: 'It feels safer not to try'

UN: 'I feel so in control when I'm restricting'

CH: 'I feel powerful'

CB: 'But when I try to eat a little bit more, I end up bingeing'

UA: 'I lose control'

Thumb: 'That's far more scary'

F1: 'It's just safer to stay as I am'

F2: 'It's safer not to try'

F3: 'I'll just keep restricting and I'll be fine'

F4: 'But I'm not sure how much longer I can keep this up'

KC: 'I think about food all the time'

TH: 'It screams to me'

EB: 'I've isolated myself from people because I can't handle the food that always goes with meeting socially'

SE: 'And besides, I have nothing of value to say anyway'

UE: 'But I feel so alone'

UN: 'No one can help me'

CH: 'I can't see a way out of this'

CB: 'I desperately want help'

UA: 'But I'm so scared of losing control'

Thumb: 'Of being made to eat'

F1: 'They'll make me be fat'

F2: 'I feel like I'm a burden to others and they'd be better off without me'

F3: 'I am freezing, I am exhausted'

F4: 'I can't go on like this'

KC: 'I am so not safe like this'

TH: 'I am not in control'

EB: 'My eating disorder is in control of me'

SE: 'My anorexia is controlling me, telling me what to do'

UE: 'I feel like I have no choice; I must do as it says'

UN: 'What will happen if I don't?'

CH: 'Can I really feel worse than I do right now?'

CB: 'Can my struggling get any worse than it already is?'

UA: 'What if I could let go of my anorexia whilst feeling in control and safe?'

Thumb: 'Would I want to?'

F1: 'What if my biggest fear about giving up anorexia could be dealt with?'

F2: 'Would that be OK?'

F3: 'What if I could feel calm and relaxed about giving up my anorexic behaviours?'

F4: 'How would that feel?'

KC: 'What if I could be helped out of that well, knowing that I wouldn't fall and hurt myself?'

TH: 'Would I try again?'

EB: 'If I could let go of my past I could change my future'

SE: 'If I could let go of the negatives I could be more positive'

UE: 'If I could feel better about myself, more confident and happy, I could kiss goodbye to Ana'

UN: 'I wouldn't need Ana to help me deal with the bad stuff in my life'

CH: 'I could deal with it myself'

CB: 'I now have a tool called EFT that I can use whenever I need to'

UA: 'I can have a life where I'm happy'

Thumb: 'I can be an even better mum'

F1: 'I can enjoy loving relationships'

F2: 'I can be even better in my work'

F3: 'I can enjoy being with friends and family again'

F4: 'I can have a better life than I ever have'

KC: 'All this is totally possible, but only if I kiss goodbye to Ana'

TH: 'It doesn't need to be scary'

EB: 'I can be in complete control'

SE: 'I can feel safe'

UE: 'I have nothing to fear'

UN: 'I just need to trust'

CH: 'I can do this'

CB: 'I want to be free'

UA: 'I deserve to be free'

Thumb: 'I choose to feel calm'

F1: 'I choose to feel relaxed'

F2: 'I choose to feel at peace'

F3: 'With myself'

F4: 'Knowing that I can do this'

KC: 'I want to do this'

Remember that these were my words based on what I was feeling when I was struggling. I want you to write down exactly how you feel and tap on this, just as I've demonstrated.

Learn to love yourself and put yourself first.

This is not selfish or egotistical.

This is essential so that you can see how much you deserve to be happy and free of Ana!

The 'What to Work On' worksheet will help you start to identify any issues that you would like to tap on. You can also download this worksheet from: www.jkp.com/catalogue/book/9781785924644.

What to Work On

1. What issue do I want to work on?

   - How am I feeling today?

   - Challenging an eating disorder behaviour such as restricting, bingeing, purging, over-exercise, using laxatives, self-harm, etc.

   - Fear of gaining weight

   - Stopping counting calories

   - Stopping weighing self

   - Fear of losing control

   - Feeling pressure from family to fight harder

   - Issues with parents/partner

   - Feeling like a mess in your job/relationships

   - Meeting a friend for coffee

   - A family event

   - An appointment

   - An argument

When I think about it, either as a future or past event, how does it make me feel NOW?

2. What is the emotion I feel?

- Anger
- Upset
- Guilt
- Shame
- Sadness
- Fear
- Anxiety

- Helplessness
- Frustration
- Doubt
- Disappointment
- Hurt
- Shock

3. Where do I feel this in my body?

4. What does it feel like?

- Racing heart
- Tight chest
- Cloud in head

- Churning stomach
- Block in throat

5. What is the level of intensity (0–10, where 0 = nothing and 10 = maximum intensity)?

Write your answers here and start tapping on them:

_____

_____

_____

_____

Now start tapping:

> 'Even though I feel [this emotion] it feels like [feeling] in my
> [where in your body] and it's a Level [1–10], I completely
> love and accept myself.'

Tap two rounds, just repeating the emotion, the feeling and where it is in your body. Then continue tapping as many rounds as necessary, talking about how you feel and your thoughts and emotions until you start to feel calmer.

Next, whilst still tapping, tell yourself that you have held on to this feeling for a long time, it has not helped and you are ready to let it go – that you want to let it go, that it's safe to let it go.

॥॥॥॥॥॥ ◆ ·◆· ◆ ॥॥॥॥॥॥

*You place so much importance
on being thinner.*

*But the people who love you would love
you no matter what, not because of how
you look but because you are you!*

॥॥॥॥॥॥ ◆ ·◆· ◆ ॥॥॥॥॥॥

Changing Your Mindset is Key

When working with clients, I find that the most common negative or limiting belief is 'I am not good enough.' Once we have this belief, it is all we seem to see. Most clients will focus on everything they have got wrong in life or think that they are not perfect and beat themselves up for it.

So, let me ask you a few questions.

- Do you feel good enough right now? If not, why not?

- What is stopping you from feeling or being good enough?

- Is it other people stopping you? Are you holding on to their comments?

- Have you ever been told that you are not good enough?

- Are you interpreting others' words or actions to mean that you are not good enough?

- Is it you stopping yourself from feeling good enough? Do you feel as if you do not deserve to feel good enough? If not, why?

- What have you done to try to feel good enough?

- Have you tried being perfect, being good, putting other people before yourself, people pleasing or being desperate for everyone to like you?

- It is still not enough though, is it? How much is enough? When will it be enough?

- Is there anything that you are good enough at?

- Do you find it hard to imagine that you have not achieved or done anything in your life?

- If you think about the facts, rather than opinion, does it change things?

- Is there a difference between achieving things and being good enough?

- Are you a good person? Are you trying to do your best?

- What will it take for you to feel good enough?

- What needs to change?

Accept that what you are doing right now is not working out for you. Accept that if you continue on the same path you have been on, nothing will change. Accept that if you make the decision now that you want things to be different, they can be different.

Life can be very difficult. We all experience ups and downs, but you need to experience the downs to appreciate the ups.

We have all had damaging experiences in the past – some worse than others – but we do not need to let these things or events define us.

I worked with one client who was sexually abused by her father when she was a young girl. Up until the point where she worked with me, this naturally affected every aspect of her life. After working together, she let go of the fear, anxiety, shame, hurt and anger that she had been feeling due to what had happened, and she could move on. She no longer carries these feelings around with her; she has set herself free. You can do the same.

As I said before, my only goal when working with clients is to change their mindset – how they see themselves and their lives. This is key, as once they can see themselves as they see their friends or other people they care about, they stop placing huge expectations on themselves. They stop punishing themselves; they relax and feel more confident and more positive.

I want you now to think about how life will be if you do not change your mindset, if you do not get rid of the belief of 'I am not good enough' or any other limiting beliefs. What is your life like right now and what are the struggles you face daily?

The following questions could help you think about what these struggles are.

- Do you struggle to focus on anything but food?

- Are you stuck in a restrict/binge cycle?

- Do you keep to a long list of rules and rituals?

- Are you full of anxiety?

- Are you being tortured by the voice in your head?

- Are you exhausted? Are you freezing cold?

- Do you often feel dizzy?

- Is your hair falling out? Do you have dry skin or brittle bones?

If you want things to change, and if you want to feel more relaxed and less tortured, you need to do things differently.

iiiiiiiiiii ◆ ·◆· ◆ iiiiiiiiiii

*Do you dislike the words
'healthy' and 'recovery'?*

*If so, use your own words – maybe something
like 'stronger' and 'more confident'.*

Make this your goal!

iiiiiiiiiii ◆ ·◆· ◆ iiiiiiiiiii

Affirmation Creation

Until now you have been looking at things negatively, but I want you to use that imagination of yours, which usually focuses on the what ifs, creating great feelings of anxiety. Try to imagine life in a more positive manner.

What would you like your life to be like, ideally? How would you like to feel about yourself? Would you like to feel:

- more confident in yourself

- more self-esteem

- more positive about yourself and your life

- good enough

- worthy

- stronger

- like you belong

- like you have a purpose in life

- special

- more relaxed?

What would it feel like? How would you be different? Would you:

- stand straighter

- smile more

- give more eye contact?

Does this feel good?

You might find this difficult, but do not give up. Think about people you admire and respect, and imagine yourself with the same characteristics. Do not worry if it does not feel believable right now. It really is possible to feel this way. Make this your goal.

Take three of the things you would like to feel, and put them into an affirmation. For example, 'I am confident, relaxed and good enough.'

Then really visualise yourself being that person. Try to feel what it is like to be that confident, relaxed person who feels good enough. Perhaps there was a time when you were this person. Use every bit of your imagination to create these feelings and really try to be that person.

Notice how you stand differently and how you look more confident and positive. Notice all the differences in yourself and repeat your affirmation to yourself for a few minutes three times a day, whilst tapping on the karate chop point. This really will make a difference, so make sure you do it every day.

IIIIIIIIII ◆ ∙◆∙ ◆ IIIIIIIIII

Where are you now?

Where do you want to be?

Decide that you want to get there.

Research your options.

Plan a possible route with detours to use if you get stuck along the way.

IIIIIIIIII ◆ ∙◆∙ ◆ IIIIIIIIII

Tapping Script for I Am Not Good Enough

I want you to think about why you do not feel good enough and where you first learned that you were not good enough. Do you remember? Have you got a memory?

I want you to think about the time you had the strongest feeling of not being good enough. Do you remember this? I also want you to think about the last time you did not feel good enough. When was that? To work on the belief of not being good enough, I want you to tap on these memories.

Let us begin with the memory of when you last felt not good enough. I am focusing on this one, as the others may be too traumatic and I do not want you to work on any traumatic memories alone – you need to do these with a practitioner.

Picture this memory in your mind, if it feels alright to do so, and try to make it as real as possible. What emotion do you feel? Where do you feel it in your body? What does it feel like? Give it a level of intensity between 0 and 10, where 0 = you feel nothing and 10 = you couldn't feel it any higher. Write this down, along with any other thoughts and details of this memory.

I will now give you an example to allow you to understand what to do. Please replace my words with your own words if mine do not resonate with you.

KC: 'Even though I feel sad that I'm not good enough, I completely love and accept myself'

KC: 'Even though I feel disappointed that I'm just never good enough, I completely love and accept myself anyway'

KC: 'Even though I feel frustrated that I'll never be good enough, I choose to love and accept myself anyway'

TH: 'I'm not good enough'

EB: 'I'll never be good enough'

SE: 'I feel so sad'

UE: 'I feel so disappointed'

UN: 'I feel so frustrated'

CH: 'I feel so angry at others for making me not feel good enough'

CB: 'My parents, friends from the past, teachers, kids from schools'

UA: 'They did and said those things to me'

Thumb: 'So I can never feel good enough'

F1: 'But why am I still holding on to these memories?'

F2: 'Memories from so long ago'

F3: 'When I was just a child'

F4: 'And that person didn't have a clue that I'd take it so much to heart'

KC: 'They've long forgotten about what happened'

TH: 'But I've been carrying it around ever since'

EB: 'Did they even say that I'm not good enough?'

SE: 'Or did I just interpret their words to mean I wasn't good enough?'

UE: 'Did I interpret them correctly?'

UN: 'Am I really not good enough?'

CH: 'What is good enough anyway?'

CB: 'I've done lots in my life'

UA: 'Trying to be perfect'

Thumb: 'Trying to be good'

F1: 'I've always put others before me'

F2: 'I'm usually the last on the list'

F3: 'I'm always people pleasing'

F4: 'I'm desperate for others to like me'

KC: 'So I'll always go the extra mile'

TH: 'How can this not be good enough?'

EB: 'Would it be good enough for others?'

SE: 'Of course'

UE: 'But not me'

UN: 'Maybe I'm stopping myself from feeling good enough'

CH: 'Do I not deserve to feel good enough?'

CB: 'How much do I need to do in order to feel good enough?'

UA: 'When will it ever be enough?'

Thumb: 'Am I good enough at anything?'

F1: 'There must be something I'm good at'

F2: 'I've achieved things in my life'

F3: 'I've done things'

F4: 'I even did some of them well'

KC: 'So why can't I feel good enough?'

TH: 'If I think about the facts, rather than my opinion of myself, does it change things?'

EB: 'What is the difference between achieving things and being good enough?'

SE: 'I'm a good person'

UE: 'I'm just trying my best'

UN: 'But why can't I let myself be good enough?'

CH: 'Do I need someone to tell me I'm good enough?'

CB: 'Would I even believe them?'

UA: 'Who makes the rules about being good enough?'

Thumb: 'What is the measurement of being good enough?'

F1: 'I'm sure I've got a different ruler'

F2: 'But why?'

F3: 'Because I chose that ruler'

F4: 'I chose to be harder on myself than anyone else I know'

KC: 'I don't feel good enough right now'

TH: 'But that doesn't mean I can't'

EB: 'I can feel good enough'

SE: 'I've gotten pretty stubborn over the years'

UE: 'I won't give myself a break'

UN: 'I won't let this go'

CH: 'But what will happen if I don't?'

CB: 'More and more years of misery and unhappiness'

UA: 'More and more years of anxiety'

Thumb: 'It's not what happens to us that defines us'

F1: 'It's how we think and feel about what's happened to us'

F2: 'How we've chosen to interpret it'

F3: 'I chose to interpret things wrongly'

F4: 'But that's OK'

KC: 'Because that means I can re-choose'

TH: 'I can change my mind'

EB: 'I can choose to feel good enough'

SE: 'I am good enough'

UE: 'Just as I am now'

UN: 'I don't need to save the world in order to feel good enough'

CH: 'It's OK to just be me'

CB: 'There's only one of me and I'm going to celebrate it!'

UA: 'I choose to feel calm'

Thumb: 'I choose to feel relaxed'

F1: 'I choose to feel at peace with myself'

F2: 'I choose to feel safe'

F3: 'I choose to feel good about myself'

F4: 'I choose to feel positive'

KC: 'Because it's the best thing for me'

Take a deep breath in and then slowly breathe out, imagining letting all the negative emotions go with your breath.

I want to make it perfectly clear that doing this tapping just once for a few minutes will probably not help much. It is only when you do it repeatedly and for several memories that it will start to make a difference.

A lot of people know how to tap but find it difficult on their own. Maybe they're not motivated enough, they need support or they're not sure what words to use.

I've worked with many different clients over the years and I've seen great transformations. If you're getting some results, consider working with a qualified EFT practitioner to help you further.

I can help you get rid of your negative beliefs and also help you make peace with your past so that you can be that person who you visualised earlier – someone who feels good enough, confident, positive, strong and so on: somebody who can kiss goodbye to Ana.

Matrix Reimprinting

Matrix Reimprinting is the next step on from EFT. EFT is amazing at helping us let go of the negative emotions we feel today; Matrix Reimprinting allows us to deal with these emotions at the time they first happen, which I have found is even more effective.

Matrix Reimprinting is an advanced form of EFT and was created by Karl Dawson. In my opinion, it can be even more powerful than EFT and I use it in the majority of my work.

This technique allows us to reprogram our minds even further so that rather than just releasing the negative emotions and beliefs, we can also replace them with positive ones.

I'm not teaching you Matrix Reimprinting here as I don't want to overwhelm you with too many techniques. For now, practise EFT and become confident in using this tool before trying to learn Matrix Reimprinting to work on yourself. I wanted to bring this technique to your attention though, so that you are aware of all the options available to you when working with a practitioner like myself.

Challenging your behaviours about
eating, food and weight can be scary.

But feeling good enough is the
key to your recovery.

So why not focus on that?!

Do not believe the voice in your head
that tells you you're bad for eating.

It's been lying to you for a long time.

Look where it's got you.

Chapter 11

DAILY REMINDERS

Use these to help you every day. Just reading them is not going to help much; you have to do the practice! You can download the daily affirmations to print and keep handy or put up around your home: www.jkp.com/catalogue/book/9781785924644.

Be Mindful Monday

- Try not to think about anything but the present moment.

- Don't think about the future.

- Don't think about the past.

- Just focus on now.

- Don't let your thoughts of anything else overtake you.

- Be present with any tasks you undertake.

- Be aware of the beauty around you as you go about your day.

- Try to make these 'now' moments the best they can be.

Challenging Tuesday

- What could you challenge yourself to do today?

- Is there anything that can potentially help you to feel good about yourself?

- Is there anything that can make you feel like you've achieved?

- Is there anything that can make you feel proud of yourself?

- It doesn't have to be big – little things are important too.

Letting Go Wednesday

- What do you need to let go of in order to feel better?
  - Negative thoughts?
  - Negative feelings?
  - Negative behaviours?
  - Negative people in your life?
- Whatever they are, try to let go of one thing today.

What's Best for Me Thursday

- What's your plan for today?
- Try to fill today with as many positive experiences as you can.
- It could be reading a book, drinking coffee at your favourite coffee shop, having a long bath, listening to music, going for a walk, meeting a friend, lots of cuddles with your children and/ or pets, or visiting your favourite local place.
- Try to do at least one and cherish the moment.

Thoughtful Friday

- Be aware of any negative thoughts that might enter your head.

- Rather than let this thought affect your mood, challenge it.

- Imagine you were in court, presenting evidence to the judge.

- Is this thought based on fact, with enough substantial evidence, or have you misinterpreted it based on your own negative beliefs about yourself?

- Replace it with a positive thought and smile to yourself.

Learn Something New Saturday

- Learning something new is a good distraction technique.

- It's also a great achievement that you can feel proud of.

- What could you learn?

- It could be something that you've wanted to do for ages or the idea might pop into your head today.

- It could be something big that might take a while, or something small that won't take too long.

- It doesn't matter either way – just give it a shot and enjoy!

Focus on the Positives Sunday

- This can sometimes be difficult to do but it doesn't mean we can't try.

- No matter what is going on in our life, there is always something we can be positive about.

- It might be hard to even feel positive about being alive, people caring about us, having a home or being able to walk, but we can try.

- Practising to focus on the positives will get easier over time, like learning a new skill.

Chapter 12

TAKE THE FIRST STEP

As someone who has recovered from anorexia and bulimia and is now qualified as an EFT and Matrix Reimprinting practitioner, I understand how difficult it is to reach out for help because of the fear of losing control and becoming fat.

I also understand now how an eating disorder is a coping mechanism and a form of staying in control because we do not feel in control of other areas of our life.

Although your thoughts may be ruled by food, this is purely a symptom; EFT can be used to discover and challenge the root cause of the eating disorder. Through this you will feel more confident, positive and good enough and no longer need to use your eating disorder to stay in control. If this root cause is not resolved, there is a tendency to use other eating disorder behaviours, such as going from being anorexic to bulimic or using another addiction entirely, such as alcoholism.

Rather than focus on your weight or food and having goals of completing meal plans and achieving goal weights, through this book and the work I do as a practitioner, I want to help you eliminate any negative beliefs you may have about yourself and any past memories that are still bothering you. My goal is to help you feel better about yourself and as good enough as everyone else.

However, there are many reasons for not wishing to recover. These may be:

- Fear of:

    ~ gaining weight

    ~ buying bigger clothes

    ~ comments from other people about weight, for example 'You look healthy / well / better'

    ~ being seen as weak if you gain weight

    ~ starting to enjoy food

    ~ others thinking you're OK and you losing their support

    ~ the unknown, for example 'I've had anorexia so long, what will it be like without it?'

    ~ facing the world as a 'recovered' person and confronting life

    ~ being unable to deal with anxiety, emotions and feelings

    ~ being unable to maintain your weight at a point you're happy with

~ being normal

~ failing – relapse is common; is it too much effort?

- Loss of:

~ a safety net – a coping method

~ your identity – who will you be without anorexia?

~ your method of punishing yourself

~ a 'friend', 'Ana' – even though she's evil, she feels like your best friend in the beginning.

The fears and anxieties listed above come under three general categories:

- food and weight

- ability to cope

- how others see you.

However, once you've worked on the root issues, these fears will no longer be troublesome. You'll:

- enjoy your life and have fun so that your focus is on being happy rather than solely on food and weight

- feel confident and strong in yourself and know you have a tool that can help you with life's stresses so that you know you can cope

- not worry about how others view you because you'll be confident in your own self-worth.

So, now for the possible reasons to recover, which you can use as your goals when focusing on your recovery. Can you add to these?

- To be free of the devil in your head.

- To be free and spontaneous in life.

- To socialise and not isolate.

- To have better relationships.

- To be happy and content, with higher self-esteem.

- To not hate yourself.

- To not hate your body but see it for its ability.

- To not feel weak, tired and cold 24/7.

- To not think about food 24/7.

- To not be in constant pain.

- To not to be calorie obsessed but be able to throw away your food diary/meal plan.

- To not feel gnawing hunger pains.

- To eat intuitively, listening to hunger cues and making sound choices.

- To enjoy treats without overwhelming shame and guilt.

- To rediscover your love of cooking and baking.

- To enjoy food.

- To teach your children to have a good relationship with food.

- To think clearly, focus and concentrate.

- To end the constant numbers battle.

- To help your other physical conditions.

- To sleep better.

- To conceive.

- To enjoy and be a better parent.

- To see your children grow up.

- To go out and eat with friends and family without avoidance, anger, anxiety and shame.

- To go to college/get a job.

- To travel and enjoy more activities.

- To inspire and help others with their eating disorder recovery.

Real recovery requires commitment and, in my experience, working with a practitioner who can help you work through the underlying root issues. However, if you choose not to work with a practitioner just yet, you can still use EFT by reading and working through the exercises/worksheets in this book to help to challenge:

- the negative voices in your head

- the obsessions/rules/rituals you have around food/exercise/weighing yourself, etc.

- the guilt and fear associated with eating

- the temptation to binge/purge

- body image thoughts and feelings.

And, finally, please remember...

- Do not listen to the voice in your head that tells you you're alone. You may be on a waiting list, but that's not because you're not ill enough; it's due to a lack of resources. Reach out to online or phone helplines if you need to speak to someone right away. They may not be able to end your struggles immediately, but just having someone to talk with, who doesn't judge and who understands, can make a difference.

- Reach out to family and friends. Don't isolate. They are desperate to help you. Trust that they're not interfering but want the best for you. You need to tell them how they can help you.

- Find an eating disorder support group either locally or online, or an eating disorder charity, as it can help to talk to others who understand and relate to how you're feeling.

And if you're really struggling right now, just for today:

- Know that you are loved and valued.

- Take each day one hour, one minute or one second at a time if that's all you can manage.

- Try to fill your day with as many positive activities as possible.

- Be kind to yourself – treat yourself as you would your best friend.

- Reach out and ask for help now.

- Don't stop looking if one option for help isn't available; keep searching.

- Remember that getting help may seem scary, but not getting help can be even worse.

- Know that you can feel better.

- Remember, true recovery isn't easy, but it is possible and it is *so* worth it!

- All the fears I had about recovery are no longer my fears.

*Just for today, are you going
to choose you or Ana?*

Because you can't choose both!

Desperate to feel lighter?

*Get rid of the huge weight of anxiety,
fear and guilt; the need to do it yourself;
and the need to be perfect, etc. that you're
constantly carrying around with you.*

References

Craig, G. (2017) 'The Writings on our wall in practice.' *Gary Craig's Official EFT Training*. Accessed on 30/09/2017 at www.emofree.com/eft-tutorial/tapping-deeper/practice.html.

Lee, H. (1991) *To Kill a Mockingbird*. London: Mandarin.

Mind (2016) *What Talking Treatments Are There?* Accessed on 30/09/2017 at www.mind.org.uk/information-support/drugs-and-treatments/talking-treatments/types-of-talking-treatments.

NHS Choices (2016a) *Treating Clinical Depression*. Accessed on 30/09/2017 at www.nhs.uk/Conditions/Depression/Pages/Treatment.aspx.

NHS Choices (2016b) *Cognitive Behavioural Therapy (CBT)*. Accessed on 30/09/2017 at www.nhs.uk/Conditions/Cognitive-behavioural-therapy/Pages/Introduction.aspx.

NHS Choices (2016c) *Borderline Personality Disorder – Treatment*. Accessed on 30/09/2017 at www.nhs.uk/Conditions/Borderline-personality-disorder/Pages/Treatment.aspx.

Further Resources

Please contact me at kim@kissgoodbyetoana.com.

You can also find me at: www.kissgoodbyetoana.com and www.facebook.com/KissGoodbyeToAna.

Join my facebook group 'EFT Tapping – Helping You with Your Eating Disorder': www.facebook.com/groups/eftforeatingdisorders.

Subscribe to my Youtube Channel: www.youtube.com/channel/UCoDTi-rci9yUSZf1W7iwwEA.

My story has been featured in BBC Hereford and Worcester, *Worcester News*, *Evesham Journal*, *Birmingham Mail*, *Evening Express* (Aberdeen), Beat (national eating disorders charity), National Eating Disorders Association, Recovery Warriors, The Mighty, Thrive Global and Huffington Post.

I have researched further resources to help you continue your reading around talking therapies, MBCT, affirmations, EFT and Matrix Reimprinting, although I strongly recommend you consult an EFT practitioner for this work. I have also included some support helplines/websites. I am in no way endorsing any of the following websites or books.

UK Support Helplines/Websites

BEAT

www.b-eat.co.uk

0808 801 0677 Helpline

0808 801 0711 Youthline

Anorexia and Bulimia Care

www.anorexiabulimiacare.org.uk

03000 11 12 13 Helpline

Eating Disorders Support

www.eatingdisorderssupport.co.uk

01494 793223 Helpline

support@eatingdisorderssupport.co.uk

US Support Helplines/Websites

National Eating Disorders Association (NEDA)

www.nationaleatingdisorders.org

1-800-931-2237 Helpline

**National Association of Anorexia Nervosa
and Associated Disorders (ANAD)**

www.anad.org

1-630-577-1300 Helpline

The Alliance for Eating Disorders Awareness

www.allianceforeatingdisorders.com

1-866-662-1235 Helpline

Suicide Prevention Hotlines

UK: Samaritans

116 123

US: National Suicide Hotline

800-SUICIDE (800-784-2433)

Talking Therapies

Mind

www.mind.org.uk/information-support

NHS

www.nhs.uk/Conditions/stress-anxiety-
depression/Pages/types-of-therapy.aspx

MBCT/CBT

Online MBCT Course

http://bemindful.co.uk

Retreat Centres and Guided Meditations

www.mbct.com

**CBT Workshop Training Booklet: Hertfordshire
Partnership University Foundation NHS Trust**

www.hpft.nhs.uk/media/1184/cbt-
workshop-booklet_web.pdf

Affirmations

Louise Hay, Hay House Publishing
www.louisehay.com/affirmations

Hay, L. and Perrin-Falquet, J. (2004) *I Can Do It: How To Use Affirmations To Change Your Life (Louise L. Hay Subliminal Mastery)*. London: Hay House.

EFT

Ortner, N. (2014) *The Tapping Solution: A Revolutionary System for Stress-Free Living*. London: Hay House.

Church, D. (2014) *The EFT Manual*. Santa Rosa, CA: Energy Psychology Press.

The Association for the Advancement of Meridian Energy Techniques (AAMET)
www.aamet.org

Gary Craig (Founder of EFT) – Free Tutorial
www.emofree.com

Dawson Church – Free Mini-manual
www.eftuniverse.com

Matrix Reimprinting

Dawson, K. and Allen, S. (2010) *Matrix Reimprinting using EFT: Rewrite Your Past, Transform Your Future*. London: Hay House.

Dawson, K. and Marillat, K. (2014) *Transform Your Beliefs, Transform Your Life: EFT Tapping Using Matrix Reimprinting*. London: Hay House.

PSTEC

PSTEC is a self-help tool to help with negative beliefs.
A free sample is available at www.pstec.org.

Your weight is one aspect of you. Your worth is made up of so much more. When you look in the mirror, stand with confidence and pride in all that you are!

Your weight is one aspect of you. Your
worth is made up of so much more.
When you look in the mirror, stand with
confidence and pride in all that you are!

Hate the way you look?

Will you ever be happy with your body?

If changing your body isn't working...maybe
it's time to change the way you see yourself?

Exercise is great for fitness, strength
and to release endorphins in our body.

But we need fuel in order for it to benefit us.

Otherwise it'll just damage us even further.

It's like trying to run with a broken leg.

You need time to heal and get stronger.

Ana is emotionally abusing you.

She won't stop.

Say goodbye now!

Index